ALSO BY NICKLAUS SUINO

The Drinking Game

101 Ideas to Kick Your Ass Into Gear
(with Ian Gray)

Budo Mind and Body: Training Secrets of the Japanese Martial Arts
(comprehensive revision of *Arts of Strength, Arts of Serenity*)

Arts of Strength, Arts of Serenity

Strategy in Japanese Swordsmanship

Practice Drills for Japanese Swordsmanship

The Art of Japanese Swordsmanship

S.E.O. and BEYOND...

How to Rocket Your Website to Page One of Google!

S.E.O. and BEYOND...

How to Rocket Your Website to Page One of Google!

Don E. Prior III
Nicklaus Suino

Ann Arbor, Michigan

Master and Fool, LLC
3853 Research Park Drive, Suite 110
Ann Arbor, Michigan 48104

Copyright © 2013 by Don E. Prior and Nicklaus Suino

Many of the activities described in this book are simple, concise and effective! However, neither the authors nor the publisher is responsible for the results of your choice to implement our suggestions. You do so at your own risk.

All rights reserved. No part of this book may be reproduced in any form or by any means, electronic or mechanical, including photocopying, recording, or by any information storage or retrieval system, without permission in writing from the authors.

10 9 8 7 6 5 4 3 2 1

FIRST EDITION

Written, Edited, and Printed in the
United States of America

ISBN: 1482585499
ISBN-13: 978-1482585490

It is not the strongest of the species that survive, nor the most intelligent, but the one most responsive to change.
- *Charles Darwin*

DEDICATION

To Amy Surakomol Prior and Pamela Suino
for their support of our efforts to rocket
EVERYBODY'S website to page one of Google

CONTENTS

Introduction — 1

Section I – What Google Wants — 4

Section II – What People Want — 7
   Identify Your Idea, Product or Service — 8
   Check Google Trends — 10
   Check the Google Adwords Keyword Tool — 12
   Focus on your Top Ten Keywords — 14
   Check the Google Adwords Traffic Estimator — 16

Section III – Choosing Your Domain — 18
   Register Your Domain for at Least 3 Years — 21

Section IV – What Robots Want — 22
   Create a Page for Every Keyword or Phrase — 22
   Create Keyword-Rich Page Titles — 25
   Use Effective Headers — 28
   Add Keyword-Rich Content — 30

Use Keyword <em> and <strong> Tags	32
Employ Four-in-One Optimization	34
Include Meta Tags	36
Craft Effective Meta-Descriptions	38
Use ALT Tags	41
Include Keyword-Rich Content Below the Fold	43
Add Potential Client Descriptions	45
Include Location Information	46
Employ Slides	48
Pay Special Attention to Your Home Page!	49
Get Connected	50
Offer Useful Articles	52
Submit Your Site	53

Section V – What Web Geeks Want — 54

Use Good Source Code	56
Avoid Prefab Website Builders	58
Use Conventional Layout	60
Eliminate Barriers	62
Add a Sitemap	64
Add an XML Sitemap	65
Use CSS for Styling	66
Don't Use Depricated Styling Tags	67
Use Keywords in Your Link Titles	68
Store Javascript and CSS Files Separately	69
Create an RSS Feed	72
Use a Server-Side Language Like PHP	73
Use a Content Management System	74

Section VI – What Marketing Experts Want   75
    Think Like a Potential Customer   76
    Know Your USP   79
    Include a Call to Action   81
    Write for the Web   82
    Under Promise and Over Deliver   84
    Include Keyword-Related Questions   85
    Offer Free Stuff   86
    Use Checklists for Engagement   88
    Add Smiling Faces   89
    Add Cute Animals   90
    Add a Pretty Girl   92
    Include a Page of Misspellings   93
    Participate in or Host a Forum   94
    Create an FAQ List   95
    Include a Top Ten List   96
    Include Funny Stuff … and Say So!   97
    Include Videos on Your Home Page   98
    Include Tutorials   99
    Incentivize Your Visitors   100

Section VII – Social Media   101
    Utilize the "Magnificent Seven" Platforms   103
    Use Powerful Social Media Strategies   106

Section VIII – Test & Measure — 123
- Use Google Analytics — 123
- Employ Custom Landing Pages — 124
- Review Your Stats — 125
- Actually Modify Accordingly — 126
- Use Eye Tracking — 128
- Check Your Backlinks — 129
- Check Others' Links to You — 130
- Be Patient — 131

Section IX – Getting on Top & Staying There! — 132
- Check Your Competitors' Sites — 132
- Tell the Search Engines What to Index — 133
- Add Regular Updates — 134
- Point Other Domain Names to Your Site — 135
- Link to Your Pages in Your Email Signature — 137
- Become an Authority Website — 139
- Read One Article a Day — 141
- Learn XHTML & CSS — 142
- Hire a Professional! — 143

INTRODUCTION

SEO stands for "Search Engine Optimization." It's the art and the science of getting your website listed higher on Google and the other search engines.

Why should you bother? Because most people today head straight for the Internet – on their computer, their phone, or their tablet – when they're trying to find something. But there are millions of businesses with websites, so simply having one of your own isn't enough for people to find you and help you become successful. If you want to be HIGHLY VISIBLE, your website must stand out from the crowd and appear on the first page of Google and the other search engines.

That's where this book comes in. There are a few major things – and many minor things – you can do to optimize your site so it appears higher in the search engines.

S.E.O and Beyond...

We've tried to make it as easy as possible, but we want you to realize going in that it isn't something you'll knock off on a Saturday afternoon. Succeeding at SEO will require a significant commitment of time and energy. So plan accordingly. Once some of the initial work is out of the way, you can go into maintenance mode and spend a few hours a week tweaking and improving the content of your website and managing your social media, and ultimately enjoying the fruits of your labor.

To simplify your work, we've broken down what needs to be done into small steps. Getting to PAGE ONE will still require a lot of planning and effort, but by tackling these steps one or two at a time, it becomes a significant, but doable project.

We also realize that not everyone has the time and energy to do SEO for themselves. If that's the situation you're in, there's no shame in asking for help. Actually, it's the smart thing to do! Once you read this book, you'll be armed with the basic knowledge of what needs to happen for success on the internet, the various tasks involved, and how they fit together. You can use this knowledge to find a web marketing or SEO expert to help you achieve your goals – someone who will do things the right way.

By the way, if you're new to website building, it's probably best to read through this whole book quickly, then start at the beginning and implement our suggestions step-by-step as you work. If you're

Introduction

more experienced, our book can help remind you of things you can do to help promote your website, so you can probably just scan the chapters and dig in where it makes the most sense.

We think most of the information in this book will help most of the people who have a website (or several websites). If something doesn't apply to you, skip it. You won't hurt our feelings (not very much, anyway). The Internet is evolving fast, and what we tell you today may not make as much sense tomorrow. Nevertheless, we're confident that the foundation we outline in this book will serve you well, and you'll see later that one of our suggestions is to make sure you spend at least a few minutes a day reading blog posts or videos by web building and SEO experts. Even though the basics don't change much from week to week, it's good to know what's going on at the cutting edge.

If you'd like more information or want to dig deeper into some of our topics, we provide a list of resources available on the internet. If you'd like a free copy, contact us! We'd love to help. You can find our contact info at:

www.seoannarbor.com

Section I – WHAT GOOGLE WANTS

This section actually consists of only one chapter. That's because knowing what Google wants is REALLY, REALLY IMPORTANT. Google accounts for the vast majority of searches, and if you focus on making sure Google likes your website and gives it a prominent position on its search results pages, you'll probably do well. At the same time, if your site works well for Google, it will almost certainly work well for the other search engines. Knowing what Google wants is the starting point for everything else you'll do on the web!

So ... What *Does* Google Want?

There's a lot of chatter out there about how Google really wants to control THE ENTIRE PLANET! (Dramatic music here). We sort of doubt that's true, but if they're listening, hey Google, can we at least have part of Hawaii? There's a great condo on Maui that we'd sort of like to keep.

What Google Wants

When it comes to what Google wants for websites, however, the answer is pretty obvious. Because it wants its search engine to be useful to web users, Google wants to do the best job possible of featuring websites that actually provide what a searcher is looking for. So, what are searchers looking for? We're putting the answer in bold letters just to help emphasize how important this is for you to understand ...

CONTENT!

Content that matches our search terms. Content that's interesting and helpful. Content that's well organized. Content that's funny. Content that's popular. Content that's easy to find. Content that doesn't try to trick or mislead.

> It's probably fair to say that if you created a website loaded with content people really, really wanted, and you were the only one who had that content, you wouldn't need to do any SEO or web marketing at all.

However, there are probably hundreds, if not thousands, of people in your field who want to succeed just like you, so chances are you're not only competing to be heard among the noise of millions of websites, you're also competing with a number of websites who offer similar ideas, products, or services. That means it's not enough to simply build a site that displays your content and wait

How to Rocket Your Website to Page One of Google!

for the visitors to pour in, even if your content is darn good. There are, in fact three general areas you have to manage to build a steady stream of visitors to your site. In a nutshell, here's what you have to do to make sure you are giving Google what it wants:

Provide Great Content
As we mentioned, you should write about what you do in a clear, compelling, original way.

Organize Your Content with a Great structure
You should organize your website in a way that's easy for people to follow and easy for the search engines to index.

Build Great Popularity
You should find ways to get the right people on the internet to talk about your website and point others to it.

There are a lot more pesky details than this, of course. You'll have to develop some specialized knowledge to compete against everybody else out there who's trying to make their sites popular, but those three points illustrate the general idea. You'll have a much better understanding of the pesky details once you read this book. So ... let's get started!

Section II – WHAT PEOPLE WANT

If a website lands on the internet and nobody sees it, is it still a website?

Philosophers may ponder that question for a millisecond or two, but what you and I need to know is whether anybody will pay attention once YOUR site is posted. Because no matter how much you love your idea, product or service, and no matter how passionately you hope that other people will love it too, you have to speak to potential visitors in a language they're already using. In this section, we'll help get you started on that process. Here are the topics we'll discuss:

- Your Idea, Product or Service
- Google Trends
- Google Adwords Keyword Tool
- Focus on Your Top Ten Keywords
- Google Adwords Traffic Estimator

S.E.O and Beyond...

Identify Your Idea, Product or Service

Nobody knows your business as well as you do! You spend every day working in your field (we hope), selling your particular brand of widget and interacting with fans, vendors or clients. So it's likely that you have a detailed understanding of the most active topics and subject areas and where the most exciting new trends can be found in your line of work. This is a good thing – it's what brings you success ... usually.

In SEO and web marketing, however, this specialized knowledge can sometimes be a handicap. We've found that even when they're great business people, our clients tend to focus on trade language, insider topics, and aspects of their business most relevant to them at the moment. They often neglect simple words and concepts more likely to appeal to the average consumer.

That's why KEYWORD RESEARCH is so important - it helps you find out what actual consumers are looking for. Once you know the keywords and phrases being searched with the highest frequency, you can make sure you're speaking in words people are actually using.

The first step in doing your keyword research is to come up with a list of words and phrases that relate to the thing or idea you're

What People Want

offering or trying to sell. If you're selling used cars, you might include words like "used cars," "vehicles," "one owner," "low mileage," or "certified." If you're a veterinarian, you might want words like "vet," "dog," "cat," "animal hospital," or "pet care." If you're selling laxatives ... well, never mind.

You get the idea, right? The point is to come up with a healthy list of keywords - words related to your idea, product or service. Get help from your employees. Ask your friends. Troll related websites. Take a few shots at it. When you have a list that seems fairly complete, go to step 2: Check Google Trends.

How to Rocket Your Website to Page One of Google!

Check Google "Trends"

A good way to get a rough idea of how many people are searching for a particular word or phrase is to use Google "Trends."

www.google.com/trends/

Trends allows you to enter up to five words or phrases (separated by commas). Your results will show the relative number of people searching for each word or phrase.

Suppose you sell floor coverings and you're trying to decide whether to focus this month's online advertising on tile, plank flooring, bamboo, or carpet (we realize this example probably seems silly if you're actually in the flooring business, but we're not the experts in your field!). You just type those words into Google Trends and you'll know which of them is being searched for most, which second, which third, and so forth. You'll have a good general understanding of the online trends. We're pretty sure that's why they call it "Trends"!

There are a few things to keep in mind both about the value of Google Trends and its limitations. Trends shows results for the entire English internet, not necessarily for your city (though it does break those results down by geographic region). It's more a butter knife than a scalpel. It's also true that just because lots of people are searching for a particular term doesn't mean they're going to find your website.

> *There are strategies on how to become successful by avoiding the most searched-for terms, but for now we'd just like you to keep in mind that Trends is more of a tool for getting to know the big picture than it is for developing a detailed keyword list for your website.*

One other neat aspect of Google Trends that can be helpful for websites dealing with hot topics or current events is that it shows spikes in searches and correlates them with major news stories. That can be very helpful if you're researching when to emphasize certain words and phrases and what information to correlate them with to take advantage of surges in search numbers. That kind of work is mostly outside the scope of this book, but some businesses thrive using that kind of data.

Once you've got an idea of the big picture, it's time to go to step 3: the Adwords Keyword Tool.

S.E.O and Beyond...

Check the Google Adwords Keyword Tool

Once you've developed your list of keywords and phrases and gotten the big picture with Google Trends, you're ready to find out what the millions of internet users are actually searching for in your field. One of the best ways to do that is to use the Keyword Tool offered by Google Adwords. You can find Adwords at:

www.google.com/adwords/

Because it's offered by Google, and because Google is by far the most-used search engine, you get up-to-the-minute results showing every imaginable search term. It even includes misspellings and keywords you may not have thought of. Most importantly, the results show what people are actually searching for rather than what you may think they're searching for. This is truly helpful ... we think it's better to be rich than to be right. Right?

For most topics, the keyword tool will give you a huge list (often around 800 results). You can sort the list by MOST SEARCHED, LOCAL SEARCHES (this is the one we use most often, because it shows what people in the US are searching for), and several other very helpful criteria. It's easy to download this list into Excel or some other data management format to help you collate the results.

What People Want

So how are you ever going to optimize your site for over 800 words and phrases? There's an easy answer to that question: you're not.

Almost nobody has the resources to optimize that many terms, and the good news is that most of us will do very well by focusing on the top ten or so words and phrases (more about that in a later chapter).

By the way, opening an Adwords account is free. Just Google "Adwords." You'll find the Adwords site in the organic listings at this address: adwords.google.com/ You can sign up for a free account, or sign up through your existing Google or Gmail account. Pretty nice for a company that wants to rule the world, huh?

Another tool to evaluate what keywords and phrases you should use is the TRAFFIC ESTIMATOR within Google Adwords. You can read more about that in Step 5: Adwords Traffic Estimator. But for the moment, let's talk about how to develop the list of keywords and phrases you should optimize. That's Step 4: Focus on Your Top Ten Keywords.

Focus on Your Top Ten Keywords

Once you've developed a list of keywords and phrases that people are actually searching for by using the Adwords Keyword Tool, you'll need to pare down the list to a manageable number. What's that number? It depends on you.

If you have a webmaster who can intelligently include keywords on the pages of your website as we are going to suggest in the following chapters, include as many as you can afford to pay him or her to optimize. If you do your own website work, go ahead and include as many as you have the time and energy to optimize.

> *But here's a word of warning: SEO and internet marketing make sense only if you are consistent, you work over the long term, and you measure your results.*

We constantly monitor the search engines to see where our clients' sites show up. We use that data to decide where to focus our efforts - if a particular keyword or phrase is not getting the results our client wants, we put more effort into that keyword or phrase. Sometimes a LOT more effort, such as writing articles, posting information on Facebook, Twitter and Youtube, asking them to host special events, creating special offers for potential customers, gathering relevant links to their webpage, issuing news releases,

What People Want

and so on and so forth. Monitoring your search engine results can take a lot of time and effort. That's why we limit the number of keywords we manage for our clients, and why you should choose a reasonable number for your website. We suggest you start with ten that are most important to your business. If you find that you can effectively manage those and still have time to run your business, you can add more later.

So take a look at the list of words generated by your keyword tool. Start by focusing only on the 100 words with the most local searches (the work involved in creating copy and monitoring results for words not in the top 100 is just not worth the effort for most of us). Next, eliminate any words that don't directly apply to your business. Then get rid of duplicates or near duplicates. There's an art to knowing exactly which words to keep and which to discard, but basically you want to try to focus on keywords that closely relate to the subject matter on your website, that you think potential visitors or customer will type into a search engine when they're trying to find an idea, product or service like yours.

Once you've got the list narrowed down to the top 10, find a place to keep that list where it won't get lost. It's VERY important to know exactly which words you're working on and to be able to keep track of your results over a long period of time. When you've got the list safely stored away, you can go on to Step Number 5: Google Adwords Traffic Estimator.

S.E.O and Beyond...

Check Google Adwords Traffic Estimator

The Adwords Traffic Estimator asks you to enter your chosen keywords and your estimated budget. It then shows you what you could expect if you were to launch an Adwords campaign with those keywords. It gives you data on how many searches you can expect, how many clicks on your ad, and what you'd pay for those clicks. This isn't a book about using Adwords to promote your business, so for now, let's focus on how the Traffic Estimator can help you decide how to use your chosen keywords.

It's really just another way to review your words and see how they stack up. The KEYWORD TOOL will let you know what words are being searched, and which have the top frequency of searches in the US. With the TRAFFIC ESTIMATOR, you will see the most popular words and their relative frequency, but you'll also get an idea of how much it would cost you to have those ads displayed in the Adwords results if you decide to advertise.

Why does that matter? Because the amount people are willing to pay tells you a lot about the competition in your field. Think about it this way: most Adwords advertisers pay from a few cents to a dollar for a clickthrough to their website. But some are willing to pay as much as $50 when somebody clicks, and if that's the case, you can bet they expect to make a lot of money off those visitors. (Some of the most expensive Adwords terms when we checked were: "insurance," "loans," "mortgage," "attorney" and "credit").

If you discover that there's a lot of competition for your keywords and you haven't already thought about whether you're in a position to compete with the really big players, this might be a good time to reflect on your business. Maybe your focus should be one or two tiers below the top players, where there's less competition for keywords, and where, in the brick and mortar world, you might not be competing against stores with giant advertising budgets.

But here's another sneaky suggestion: if you find out that the most searched terms in your field are very, very competitive, and you're sure that's the business you want to be in, then find out who the top few players are, and become a student of their websites. What keywords are they focusing on? What online marketing do they use? What other websites are linking back to theirs? How are they using social media? It's very likely that they are doing several things right, and learning what those things are could make a big difference for your business.

By now, you should have a Top Ten Keyword list and you should know how competitive those keywords are. Let's go on to the nuts and bolts of SEO on your website!

Section III – CHOOSING YOUR DOMAIN

What's in a [Domain] name? You'd think choosing name of your website would be easy. You just take the name of your business, reserve MYBUSINESSNAME.COM, build a website, and the millions start to flow in.

Except it doesn't quite work that way.

We're betting that even if your business been around a long time, there are a lot of potential customers who don't know its name. They may know that they suddenly need left handed widgets or a peanut-butter infused scalp rinse, but if they haven't done business with you before, they probably won't type MyBusinessName.com into Google. Instead, they'll type something like "left handed widgets Baltimore" (if they live in Baltimore), or "peanut butter scalp rinse Rochester" (if they live in Rochester).

Choosing Your Domain

This is important. We've seen this mistake made over and over again, and for some reason even otherwise very savvy business people have trouble understanding the idea. Unless you're one of of the top 1 – 3 brands in your field (like Apple, Nike, or Delta), people don't search for the name of your business. They search with words that describe the idea, product, or service that they want.

> *If you've chosen MYBUSINESSNAME.COM for your website and your business name doesn't contain words that describe your idea, product or service, you're potentially losing a huge number of website visitors.*

Since you're one of the thousands of smart people reading this book, however, you're already armed with the knowledge of what people are *actually* using to search for your idea, product, or service. If you want to get the maximum power for your website, choose a domain name that contains a commonly searched keyword or phrase that you discovered in your research process. If your business is local, add the name of the city where your customers shop. Here are some real world examples:

SEOANNARBOR.COM
Contains both the service [SEO] and the location [Ann Arbor].

NETWORKSERVICESGROUP.COM
Contains the service [network services].

How to Rocket Your Website to Page One of Google!

ANNARBORARMS.COM
Contains both the location [Ann Arbor] and the product [arms].

JAPANESEMARTIALARTSCENTER.COM
Contains the product/service [Japanese martial arts].

COLORADOATTORNEY.COM
Contains the location [Colorado] and the service [attorney].

Does that help you see how some businesses solve the domain name problem? By the way, if you've already got a website that uses your business name, and that name doesn't contain important keywords, it's not too late. You can always reserve an additional domain containing those keywords and point it to your existing website. Over time, you'll want to migrate all your content to the new domain name. That way, you won't lose any of the customers who are already finding you using your business name.

If you absolutely, positively don't want to change your domain name, it's not the end of the world. There are ways to boost the prominence of the pages of your website using page names, headers, content, and tags, and dozens of other ways which we'll talk about in detail in the coming chapters. Just remember, if you have any competitors at all, they're thinking about ways to boost their prominence, too. If their websites suddenly appear on Page One of Google and yours doesn't, don't say we didn't warn you!

Register Your Domain for at Least Three Years

By the way, when you register your domain name – like www.nickswidgets.com - you might be better off registering it for three or five years or so instead of one year. Some experts say Google's search engine algorithm may take into account the length of time for which your domain is registered. The idea behind this was that Google was supposedly trying to figure out which domains represented serious businesses, and which were just for fly-by-night operations.

Other experts disagree that domain registration has any effect on search engine performance, and at one time Google even reported that it didn't take this into account. However, registering domains is so cheap that you might as well go for five years just in case Google is being sneaky!

Section III – WHAT ROBOTS WANT

Create A Page for Every Keyword or Phrase

Suppose you have an auto repair shop that specializes in providing service for European imports such as Audi, VW, and BMW. When people go to Google and search for "bmw auto repair ann arbor" you'd like your site to show up on Page One and, if possible, near the top of Page One. Right?

Further suppose your current site has a "services" page that mentions your work on BMW, VW, Audi and other imports, but you have no page specifically for "bmw auto repair ann arbor." Are you beginning to see the problem? Even while hoping to be featured in the search results for a very specific phrase, you don't have a page designed for that purpose. But your competitor does. Whoops!

The solution is to create a specific landing page just for "bmw auto repair ann arbor." Yes, you should go so far as to make sure the filename of the page includes those keywords. In other words, the URL should look something like this:

http:// website.com/bmw_auto_repair_ann_arbor.html

The HTML title of the page should also contain those keywords (more on page titles later). The page should contain a lot of text that contains the phrases BMW, auto repair, and Ann Arbor. Each one of those phrases should also be included in an HTML H1 header tag, which we'll explain in detail a little later on.

Make sure you try to include some specific information as to what advantages your facility would offer to someone with a BMW. Do you have a BMW certified technician on staff? Make sure you understand your own USP (unique selling proposition) and communicate it to your visitors. We'll talk a lot more about that later in our secton on What Marketers Want, but the question you need to ask is what makes you so good at repairing BMW's as compared to anyone else? The more information you can provide, the more opportunities there are for you to include keywords. That will help improve the relevance of your site for those particular words and phrases.

S.E.O. and Beyond...

Keep in mind that you should always be trying to appeal to two very different visitors to your site. The first kind is the one everybody thinks of – your potential customer. We suspect your customers are mostly human beings, so your site should be easy to read and, as we've been saying, should contain a lot of helpful content. A few compelling photos and a clear layout help a lot, too, and we'll talk more about these later.

But much of what we do in SEO is designed to appeal to the other kind of visitor – the search engine robots (sometimes called "spiders" because they "crawl" websites looking for keywords). These are the software programs that the search engines have in place that check all the websites to decide which are important and which relate most closely to people's searches. The spiders only pay attention to text - not photos, pretty colors or flash animation - and that's why you want to make sure you have lots of keyword rich text on your site.

So here's the key point of this chapter: ultimately, you should create at least one page for every one of your target keywords and phrases.

Now let's go on to the next step: Page Titles.

Create Keyword-Rich Page Titles

Part of making your site relevant to search engines for your desired keywords is to make sure those same keywords are pervasive throughout your site. In other words, they should appear everywhere you can reasonably fit them: in the domain name, in content, in headers, and yes – you guessed it – in page titles!

What is a page title? Why, it's the title of the page! (Sorry).

If you look at the top of your browser window, you'll see the page title (sometimes called the page "name"). It's not exactly the same as the URL (that collection of goofy letters, words, and backslashes in the address bar, which we'll talk about in a moment). Instead, it's the set of words or phrases right at the top of the window that states, in plain language, what the page is supposed to be about. If you just go to the Google search screen, you'll notice that the page title is "Google." They can be that terse because they're Google. The rest of us have to try a bit harder.

By the way, every page on your site is really just a file stored somewhere on your web server. Often the home page is called something like Index, Home, or Default (whatever your web server is set up to serve as the default page). However, other pages will usually have highly unique names such as About, or Products <sarcasm>.

How to Rocket Your Website to Page One of Google!

The problem is, those names don't tell the search engines much about the specific content on those pages.

> *HOME ... is a lousy name for your home page!*

To amp up your SEO results, consider changing some or all your page names – or adding new pages – to include your targeted keywords and phrases. Here are some examples:

Change "**About**" to "**About Left Handed Widgets.**"
Change "**Products**" to "**Our Left Handed Widgets.**"

For local results add a new page called "Left Handed Widgets Your City." Add a similar page for each region or area from which you want to get business.

If you're bit more technical minded, we'll point out that the "page titles" we are referring to are also HTML titles. These are made up of textual information enclosed by HTML tags, like this: <title>YOUR KEYWORDS</title>. Here's an example that contains both keywords and location information: <title>Left Handed Widgets – ACME Manufacturing – Ann Arbor, Michigan</title>

If you're using a graphical website application like iWeb or WYSIWYG Web Builder, follow their instructions for creating page titles, and make sure you include keywords wherever possible.

If you or your web programmer use HTML, you can just insert the titles that way.

If you research this, you'll see many SEO experts insist that Google reads only 66 characters. The truth is, no one knows for sure, and Google isn't saying. Our own research suggests that Google ignores titles longer than 60 or 70 characters, so our recommendation is to include enough to make sure your titles make sense and don't fail to include your primary keywords. Just make sure the most important keywords are listed first, and list each keyword only once.

And remember, each page can have its own unique title! That helps you spread your most important keywords across many pages.

Use Effective Headers

Your keywords and phrases should appear at least once in a header tag on each page dedicated to those keywords. Robots give a little more weight to headers over normal text, and HTML includes a half a dozen "header" tags (<h1> through <h6>) that allow you to structure your page in outline form. Text contained within the header elements is considered more important. Here are some examples:

<h1>Search Engine Optimization – Ann Arbor</h1>

<h2>Left Handed Widgets</h2>

Make sure you also include relevant location information in the headers if that is pertinent to your business. You might be happy to sell a widget to someone from Albuquerque, but if the vast majority of your business comes from San Diego, make sure you include <h3>San Diego</h3> along with your keywords and phrases. If you are using a web layout program, check to see how you can identify headers in the pages you create.

Just be aware that by default, the H1, H2, and even H3 tags are styled to appear... a little big. But don't let that stop you! You can style them to look any way you want by using CSS (which we'll talk about in a later chapter). The more you learn about how to design and code your own web pages, the more flexibility you'll have. But even if you have somebody else do your coding, these tips will help you have an intelligent conversation about how to promote the site.

What we want you to take away from this chapter is the simple idea that you should find ways to make sure your most important keywords are found in header text.

Add Keyword-Rich Content

Content, of course, is king! It's the reason why people come to your website, and it's the stuff the search engines are looking for when they decide how important your site is. Writing engaging, web-friendly content is both an art and a science, but the one certainty about it is that it must contain your keywords. Lots and lots of keywords!

Well, actually it's not that important to have huge numbers of keywords. It's more important to make sure they appear in all the places we've talked about (domain names, page titles, and headers), as well as a reasonable number of times in your main content.

Content can be a lot of things. It can be articles, descriptions, testimonials, questions and answers, lists, or any other text that is both interesting to visitors and useful for the search engines. We emphasize the word *text* here because we want to make sure you understand that photos, art, videos, and Flash animation cannot be read by the search engine spiders, so while they may help you attract or entertain visitors, they won't necessarily help you get your website to Page One of Google.

What sort of text should you use? Whatever makes sense on a given page. For example, on your home page it might make sense to introduce your business, describe your ideal customer, or offer a solution to a problem faced by your ideal customer. If you sell products, you can write a description of each of your products on a page. If you're promoting an idea, you can write about each aspect of that idea on a page. If people send you testimonials, post those on a "testimonials" page. If there are no keywords in the testimonials, you can introduce each one with a keyword-rich lead in, like this: "Here's what Happy Customer Joe from Our City says about our Left Handed Widgets …." In that way, you can include both location information and product keywords in your page content.

Next, let's talk about keyword <em> and <strong> tags.

S.E.O. and Beyond...

Use Keyword <em> and <strong> Tags

We've just talked about making sure your keywords are contained in the main content of your pages. You can attract the eye of your reader and give a little more weight to the search engine robots' opinion of your keywords by making sure they're emphasized. In HTML, the words can be enclosed in <em> tags for italics, or <strong> tags for bold. Here's how that would look:

<em>italicized keyword</em>

<strong>bolded keyword</strong>

Most browsers will simply style these as shown here, but if you or your webmaster understand how to use CSS, you can override the default styles and have them appear any way you see fit. The added oomph you get with the search engines when using these tags will still exist even if the words appear in a different style.

If you're using a web layout program rather than programming in HTML, just use the text editor to put your keywords in italics or bold as you see fit. If you're a little bit technical, you can view the source code of your completed pages and look for the <em> and <strong> tags.

One word of caution: some overzealous business owners get carried away and emphasize virtually everything on their websites. As far as we can tell, Google pays attention to tricks and penalizes websites when they seem be trying to gain rank without adding value to the human visitors. It's not that hard to emphasize words that truly are keywords, and because they're actually distinct from the other words on the page, we think you'll get more benefit from doing it that way.

Got it? Great! Let's go on to talk about 4-in-1 optimization.

Employ Four-in-One Optimization

Let's recap what we've talked about in the last few sections. For each of your targeted keyword or phrases, you should make sure to do the following:

> 1. Include them in the URL for that page:
> http://seoannarbor.com/four_in_one_optimization.php
>
> 2. Include them in the <title> tags:
> <title>Four in One Optimization</title>
>
> 3. Include them in the header <h1> elements:
> <h1>Four in One Optimization</h1>
>
> 4. Include them within the main page content, whether it's an article, a list, a set of testimonials, a product or service description, an explanation, a company update, or whatever primary information appears on your page.

Whatever you do, create a page for each of your targeted keywords and make sure your four-in-one optimization is complete! There are many, many more steps you can take to boost the prominence of your website, but these are the fundamentals, and they can often get you close to where you want to go, even with just a little application of all the other activities we talk about in this book.

By the way, the first guy we heard using this term (actually, he calls it "four FOR one optimization") was our friend Charly Caldwell II, a major player in the internet marketing business. If you have a business in south Florida, or if you're looking for a very engaging and informative speaker for an event anywhere in the US, contact Charly. He's one of the most valuable people we've spent time with. You can find him at:

http://www.successacademy.us/

In the meantime, let's go on to talk a bit about meta tags and ALT tags.

Include Meta Tags

HTML Meta tags are special tags that appear near the beginning of your HTML source code (the code behind your web page) that can be used to help clue the search engines in on the content of your site. They appear in the <head> section and look something like this:

> <head>
> <title>This is the page title - not a meta tag</title>
> <meta name="description" content=**"This is the meta description tag. Use this tag to provide a brief description of the content of your site. In some cases this info will appear with your listing as it is displayed in the search engines"** />
> <meta name="keywords" content="this, would, be, a list, of your, keywords, separated, by, commas" />
> </head>

There are other meta tags, but the ones listed above are the two most associated with SEO. You should use the description meta tag to provide a reasonable description of your site. It should be one or two sentences and should be well written and compelling. Since this information is often displayed in Google as the text snippet describing your site, it's worth spending time carefully crafting it. More about this later!

The meta keyword tag is used to provide search engines with a list of keywords that you feel are appropriate to your site. Ten years ago this was an effective way to tell the search engines what your site was about. However, since it runs on the honor system, people didn't play nice and tried to game the system by including popular keywords that had nothing to do with their site. It didn't take long for the search engines to figure this out, so the importance of this tag has been greatly reduced.

Despite the fact that not all search engines will pay attention to them, you should include meta tags for those that do. Working on them will help you think about and develop your list of keywords, so it is at least useful in that regard.

Craft Effective Meta-Descriptions

When most people think of meta tags, they think of keywords and the meta tags we discussed a moment ago that allow you to tell the search engines what your website is about. However, there's another important meta tag used to supply a description of your site. Unlike meta keywords, the meta-description IS used by many search engines to display summary information about your site.

This is more important than it may seem at first glance. You know how you do a Google search and find a list of websites that may potentially suit your needs? Google and the other search engines usually supply a short summary. Make sure your meta-description contains relevant and compelling information. After all, it's one thing to have your site appear high in the search engine listings, but quite another to increase the number of searchers who become actual visitors. And, as we'll discuss in later chapters, yet another matter to make sure they find useful and compelling information once they reach your site so that they take the action you're hoping they'll take.

For example, if you search "search engine optimization ann arbor," the first listing in the organic results is SEO Ann Arbor. The listing looks something like this:

What Robots Want

> *Search Engine Optimization Ann Arbor. Search Engine Optimization (SEO) can help your website appear more prominently in the various Internet Search ...*

So you've found a site that's potentially interesting, but you haven't actually clicked on the link. What you read in the text snippet could help you decide if the site will provide what you're looking for.

When we first built our site, we were hoping that, since you're searching for SEO in or around Ann Arbor, the phrase "search engine optimization can help your website appear more prominently in the various Internet Search ..."

But, upon reading that, we thought about what's contained in that snippet and realized that it could be better. If you're already looking for SEO, you probably know what it is and why you're looking for it. So it would likely be more compelling to you to see something that advances your knowledge or presents an opportunity that might help you. If you decide to check up on us, don't be surprised if our meta description has changed!

S.E.O. and Beyond...

You should engage in this same sort of thinking when you craft your own meta description. What has your potential visitor typed into the search bar to find a listing that includes your site? What does that search term tell you about their state of mind? What can you say in a short sentence or two that both informs a person in that state of mind and also helps them take the next step in their search process?

Use ALT Tags

A web page without pictures? Pretty boring, right? In fact, even Google thinks so. Google likes to return relevant results, people like web pages with pictures, and Google knows this, so including some pictures on your pages is a good thing.

However, while you and I may understand the relevance of a picture simply by looking at it, Google doesn't. Computers know how to display images, but they have no idea of what those images represent unless you clue them in. And if you're truly interested in reaching people, remember that sight-impaired people can't see the images on your site either.

There are 2 ways to let the robots and the sight-impaired know what your image are about:

> #1) Make sure the file name of your image contains keywords. For example, use "left_handed_widget.jpg" as opposed to "image01.jpg."
>
> #2) Use ALT tags!

Alt tags are optional HTML attributes that you can include along with your images to describe the images. If you're selling "left handed widgets" you probably should have a picture of one somewhere on your page. If you do, make sure you include an ALT tag with the image so that the search engines know that image is of a "left handed widget."

<img alt='left handed widget' src='img/left-handed-widget.jpg' />

Moreover, the navigation buttons on a site are often composed of images. This makes them look fancy, but doesn't communicate to either the robots or to the sight-impaired. If that's the case for your site, you should make sure you include ALT tags to describe the buttons' destination (e.g. "home page" for the home page graphic).

Include Keyword-Rich Content Below the Fold

If you've done things properly, you've hired an expert web designer to create a clean and attractive web site instead of your cousin's 17 year-old nephew who flunked algebra but fancies himself a web designer (remember those drawings he made when he was a kid, and now you have him designing you a website?).

And now that you finally have a nice clean professional design, here comes some SEO guy telling you to clutter it up with all kinds of additional text for keywords, phrases, and locations. If this troubles you, however, ask yourself this question: What good is your web site with the wonderful design if no one ever sees it?

The good news is that, while you absolutely need this stuff to increase your search engine presence, that doesn't mean your site has to become a cluttered mess. Our *first* recommendation would be to find ways to include the keywords you need in the page content itself.

But ... if including this information will clutter your site or interfere with a critical aesthetic aspect, simply place it "below the fold." That's at the very bottom of your page, where it usually says "Web Design By..." and the background color changes from what's used in the content area to what is used on the rest of the page.

S.E.O. and Beyond...

That's right, scroll waaaay down to the very bottom and put this stuff there. Most visitors will probably never even scroll down to see it, but that's not our first priority! We aren't putting it there for them – we're really putting it there for the search engines (which really don't care that it's at the bottom and in a different color).

We do need to add one cautionary note, however. There's an old "black hat" SEO technique from the 1990's that involved adding text that was the SAME color as the background. Often web designers would place text there that was not necessarily as helpful as it should be (like the names of competitors' businesses). That's NOT what we are suggesting here. Our goal, as always, is to make your website as helpful as possible within your specific subject matter, both to human eyes and to the search engine spiders.

Add Potential Client Descriptions

Does your business offer products and services that target a specific audience? For instance, is your product especially useful for attorneys, realtors, or bankers? If so, make sure you include a list of your target audience so that anyone searching for "left handed widgets for attorneys" will be more likely to find you.

You could write something like this: "We proudly offer custom made left-handed widgets for attorneys, realtors and bankers, as well as a special extreme widget for mountain bikers, snowboarders, base-jumpers and skydivers." You've helpfully explained who your product will work for as well as given the search engines some content to help them provide results for those specific targets. If you're worried about cluttering up your design with all these potential client types, put the list "below the fold."

Better yet, link each one of the items in your target audience list to a page that contains additional information on your product and how it's relevant to your target audience. This is yet one more opportunity for you to create additional keyword rich pages on your site. Each page should include plenty of keyword-rich text and 4-in-1 optimization. Synergy baby!

Include Location Information

Make sure you include relevant location information on your pages if it's pertinent to your business. While you might be happy to sell a widget to someone from Albuquerque, if the vast majority of your business comes from Birmingham, then make sure you include "Birmingham" along with your keywords and phrases, and find a way to do it on every one of your pages.

If your business is more regional in nature, make sure you include all the cities, towns and counties where you have a good chance of getting business from. That way someone searching for Cat Containers in Chicago will be more likely to find your site even if you're in Dolton, Illinois, just on the outskirts of Metropolitan Chicago.

Of course, there are limits. Just as you should winnow down your keywords so you can focus on those that are truly most likely to bring motivated people to your website, you should only focus on the top locations you hope your visitors will search for.

Including dozens of locations on each of your pages could possibly clutter up your site, but as we mentioned a moment ago, there are ways to do it where you can minimize the impact. This is another kind of information you can try placing "below the fold" – which should help retain the delightful appearance of your site while still providing critical information for those who search for your idea, product or service in a particular location.

By the way, when you've had your website for a while and have carefully tracked where your visitors come from (and what search terms they're using), you can really start to focus with a laser-like intensity on the exact searches that will attract the kinds of visitors you want. If your best left-handed widget customers come from the south side of Columbus, Ohio, particularly Grove City, Westland, and Hilltop, wouldn't it make sense to build key phrases around those locations? We'll talk a lot more about determining who your best customers are and how to reach them in our sections on marketing and social media, but for now, we just want you to recognize that it may be important to include keywords related to the locations where your potential customers are going to shop.

Employ Slides

Ideally, you want to keep the amount of clutter on your pages to a minimum, especially your home page. But sometimes you have a lot of things to promote. Another way to reduce clutter is to use rotating content, such as a slideshow, to include a lot of different items but only display one at a time.

There are many different ways to do this, but some of the better ones involve using a javascript library called "jquery." If you search Google you can find many plug-ins and small scripts that are based on jquery that allow you to include rotating content on your pages. And many of these will allow you to rotate text along with images, which is what you want. Remember, text is what will help you for search engine purposes. If you want to include a pretty picture to make things look better, go ahead and do so, but keep the size reasonable (otherwise your pages will load slowly), and avoid using Flash or Java content unless there is a compelling reason to do so (one such reason might be to display a video).

The great thing about doing this is that Google and the other search engines will see each "slide" as a block of keyword rich text, while visitors will only see one slide at a time, thus reducing clutter. It's a win-win scenario!

Pay Special Attention to Your Home Page!

Special consideration should be given to your home page because … well … it's your home page! More people will probably see it than any other page on your site. It's also the first thing the search engines see. Make sure it clearly indicates WHAT YOU DO and WHERE YOU DO IT. At a minimum, be sure to include these items:

> Keyword-rich description of your idea, product or service.
>
> Location information.
>
> Target audience description.
>
> Reduce or eliminate the need to scroll down. Display your main message "above the fold."
>
> Use slideshows or rotating content to reduce clutter.
>
> Include additional content such as geographic location and target audience "below the fold."
>
> Add additional keyword-rich text below the fold.

Get Connected

One of the most important aspects of optimizing your site for SEO purposes is getting other relevant sites to link back to yours. There are many ways to do this, such as including compelling content and articles people find so useful that they link back to you, as well as seeking out other sites for reciprocal links.

Google and the other search engines consider each link to your site as a vote of confidence. There's a science to link sharing, however, so keep in mind that not all votes are created equal. Links from more popular sites (sites with a higher page rank) have greater weight than less popular sites. The most beneficial links you can have come from relevant sites; i.e., those whose content is closely related to yours.

How do you get sites to link to yours? The best way is to have first rate content so compelling that people tell one another about it and voluntarily link to your site. But until you manage to hit that particular home run, there are a few more pedestrian ways to get the job done. First, ask your customers, vendors, tenants, friends, and acquaintances to link to your site. Having a page where you can post reciprocal links (e.g. you link back to their sites in return) can be an added motivation (you win when they link to you, and they win when you link to them).

What Robots Want

Beyond that, you can search around the Internet for other sites that might be willing to link back to your site in exchange for a reciprocal link. Just make sure you aren't linking into a "link farm" (sites that are created explicitly for generating links). That can get you in trouble with Google. Instead, link only to legitimate websites, preferably with a page rank of 3 or above, and preferably with content that is closely related to your idea, product or service.

As we mentioned above, getting "backlinks" is a science, and can involve a lot of work. There are linking specialists who spend their entire workday studying the best way to get links, the best kinds of links to get, and whether or not it makes sense to swap links with other sites. We offer link work to our clients as part of our overall approach to helping them prosper on the internet. To paraphrase the old cereal ads, link gathering is an important part of a complete breakfast!

> *Warning: sites that claim to be able to get you thousands of links for a single low fee (like $100) are probably scams. There's no way anybody can afford to spend the time getting you a large number of highly-ranked, relevant links for $100. Link building takes time and discrimination, and if you're serious about getting your site well placed, you'll find a way to commit the time and resources to do it right.*

Offer Useful Articles

According to Google, the best way to boost your site's rank is to make it useful and relevant for the keywords you hope to attract. How do you make your site relevant? Post first rate content.

If you offer truly helpful knowledge presented in an interesting way, visitors will flock to your site to see it. If you happen to sell carpet and tiles, you should post articles about the different types, what works best in certain situations your customers might face, how to install them, and so forth. If the information you're providing is truly useful, then people will not only come to see it they'll share it, and some will link back to your site. And if you keep posting updated, interesting, useful information over time, people are going to be more likely to come back on a regular basis.

As you write or gather content, keep in mind some of our earlier suggestions for posting it. Focus on a single keyword or phrase, and make sure you're informing your visitors about that specific topic. Post the article on a single page of your site, make sure you have a menu of all your articles with a live link to each one, and make sure you complete 4-in-1 optimization for every one of those pages. And, as we'll discuss in later chapters, make sure you use social media and other strategies to direct potential visitors to those pages.

Submit Your Site

Here's an easy step that a surprising number of do-it-yourself website builders (and even a few professionals!) forget: submit your site to the search engines!

When you build a new site, there's no automatic reason for Google and the other search engines to recognize that it's there. They will find it eventually, especially if other sites begin to link to yours, but for most businesses, time is money, and you want your site to appear near the top of the Google results page as soon as possible. So don't delay. Once you've built and posted the majority of your website pages, submit your domain name to search engines. Here's where you need to go to submit:

> http://www.google.com/submityourcontent/
>
> http://bing.com/toolbox/submit-site-url
>
> http://search.yahoo.com/info/submit.html

Section V – WHAT WEB GEEKS WANT

Content is king. But is it the *only* thing that matters when you're trying to get your website to page one? No! There are at least a dozen major things, and several dozen minor things, you can do to optimize your site so it appears higher in the search engines. And while content is king, some of these "things" that you can (and should) do involve web design, programming, and other technical skills. Welcome to the world of web geeks!

If you aren't a programmer, web developer, or someone who has aspirations to be one, you probably aren't going to like this, but we've seen it time and time again. The technical aspects of your site can have an adverse effect on your search ranking. If the code behind your site is messy, loads slowly, or doesn't follow convention, it can confuse the search engines and make it so they can't properly index your site.

What Web Geeks Want

That's where this chapter comes in. We'll tell you what's important and why it matters, what to avoid and what to watch out for. Whether our advice is for you, your webmaster, or your favorite web geek, this chapter will guide you through the process. Don't want to deal with it, or need some help? No worries – we're here to help. It's what we do, and there's no shame in calling in an expert.

Use Good Source Code

Behind the nice pictures and words on your website there's something called "source code." It's the strange language that programmers use to tell your browser what to show you. It does a lot of other things, too.

You can see what the source code of your page looks like, or what any page looks like, for that matter. When you're looking at a website, go to the "View" menu and choose "Page Source." If you're not into coding or html, you'll probably want to close the page source window quickly and get back to looking at your web page. That stuff's for programmers!

Good source code is clean and concise, without bugs. It ensures that your web pages load quickly. When you hire someone to design a website for you, make sure they can tell you whether they'll hand code your site in HTML or use page layout software. If somebody is charging you to design your website and they say they're going to use page layout software to do it, make sure they're using a professional design system and not one of those that tout themselves with a tagline like "design your own website in minutes!"

So keep in mind that one of the things they should be checking is whether your source code is any good. If they don't at least raise the topic, you might want to consider a different SEO firm. At SEO Ann Arbor, when we undertake to help someone, we always evaluate their source code to make sure it doesn't hinder their search engine results.

Avoid Prefab Website Builders

As we alluded to in the last section, the best way to create web pages is to have them hand coded by a skilled HTML expert. Good, clean, semantically correct HTML code is the goal, because clean code helps your page load faster, is easier for the robots to browse, and prevents functional errors. Many of the prefab website building tools create redundant code or otherwise insert errors because of the way they have to manage the information you add and the layouts you create.

If you're inclined to do it yourself, get the clean code you need by writing it "by hand" using a text editor. Yes, it's more work, but it's also the best way to get results. Try to avoid using prefab web layout tools, especially old clunky ones like Frontpage. If you look at the source code that this particular program generates you'll understand why. Some tools are better than others, such as professional grade programs like Adobe Dreamweaver, but you'll still maintain better control over your source code if you write it by hand rather than letting a prefab utility decide how it should be done. Knowledge of HTML can only help you optimize your site, and the only way to use some of our tips is to go under the hood and edit things yourself. Even if you don't become an expert in HTML, having a working knowledge of web programming can help you best utilize the skills of your webmaster.

What Web Geeks Want

We understand that not everybody has the time, money, or inclination to learn HTML. If you're one of those people, it IS better to use a prefab layout system than to have no website at all. There are many cheap or free systems available like iWeb, Wordpress, or one of the systems offered by web hosting services. If that's what it takes for you get your website out there, then go for it!

We just want you to recognize the limitations of those systems. You could spend a lot of money promoting a site built with one of those systems and find you're not getting good results. Before you do that, we hope you'll spend a little time analyzing the way your current site is coded, and do a little shopping around. If you find someone with a good reputation who can hand code a new site for you, any money you spend on optimization, link partners, and social media after that will probably result in a much higher return. And when you've made millions with your new site, you can call us to brag!

How to Rocket Your Website to Page One of Google!

Use Conventional Layout

When we say "layout", we are really talking about two different, but related things:

> #1) The overall look and feel of your site
>
> #2) The code behind the scenes used to implement your look and feel, and that makes it work in a web browser.

Taken together, these two aspects comprise what we refer to as the "layout" of your website.

Let's start by considering the look and feel of your site. We all want our sites to look great, but it's all too common for people to fall into the trap of being obsessed with appearance. The truth is, it almost doesn't matter what your site looks like as long as it contains useful, relevant and compelling content. After all, a great looking site with lousy content isn't going to attract many visitors.

So while it definitely makes sense to spend some time and energy developing a site that doesn't look awful, it's important to keep things in perspective and focus your time and energy where it will make the most difference for attracting visitors and getting them to engage with you.

What Web Geeks Want

Here's an example of what can happen when people spend too much time focusing on the look of their sites and not enough time on the content and functionality:

http://theoatmeal.com/comics/design_hell

It's a funny story, so if you get a moment, you really should go look at it! Meanwhile, let's approach this subject from another angle. Think about some of the most popular and successful websites, such as Google, Amazon, or Apple. What adjectives come to mind to describe these sites? *Simple. Clean. Attractive. Functional.* Clearly the visual layout of these sites didn't interfere with their success. We recommend starting with those adjectives when planning your own site design.

Far more important is the content that is contained on your site, and that should be the focus of your obsession. Having the best looking site in the world won't do you any good if no one visits it. You're reading this book, so our keen deductive reasoning leads us to believe that you're interested in promoting your website, having it featured prominently in the search engines, and exposing it to the widest possible audience. For that reason, we suggest that you use a simple, conventional layout unless you have a very compelling reason to do otherwise.

Eliminate Barriers

As we just discussed, HTML is the language that is used to create web pages. It started off as a simple markup language, but over time more and more features were added, making it more and more complex. The good news is that it still isn't rocket science, but it is complex enough to cause some headaches.

We've suggested that you use good, clean, semantically correct code, but what does this mean? Basically, it means that you're following the rules for modern CSS and XHTML. You can use a free service such as the W3C HTML validation service to make sure that your site is following all the rules. You can find the validator at:

http://validator.w3.org

As we've noted before, web pages can be created using other technologies such as Flash and Java, but not every web browser knows how to display them. For instance, Flash sites will not work on all computers, and will certainly not work on iPhones, iPads, and many other popular mobile devices. That's bad enough by itself (because it limits the exposure of your site) but you should also realize that the search engines can't index content that is contained within Flash and Java files, which even further limits your exposure and potential audience.

What Web Geeks Want

Whether someone's using a phone, a tablet, or a computer, they'll be viewing your web page through a web browser, and the one thing that every web browser understands is how to display proper HTML web pages.

Our advice? Use standards compliant HTML for your site and avoid proprietary third-party technologies such as Flash and Java unless there is a compelling reason to use them. Everyone with an iPhone will thank you, and so will Google when it actually recognizes the content on your site and lists you higher in its index because of it.

Doing so will get you a site that loads faster, displays properly across different browsers, is easier to maintain, and is easier for the search engines to understand and digest. Time and time again, we see sites with messy code that aren't indexed properly by the search engines, severely limiting their results. Don't let it happen to yours!

Add a Sitemap

What's a sitemap? It's a page on your site that lists all the other pages, links to them, and gives your viewers a little information about what they'll find on each one. There might not be a billion reasons why you need a site map, but there are more than you can fit inside a politician's conscience.

For example, a site map provides your viewers a place to go when they can't figure out how to navigate to the information they want on your site. It gives you yet another place to add your target keywords. It gives you a whole lot more links between pages. And it's expected by people who pay attention to whether your site is professionally designed and constructed.

For best results, make sure that each listing in the site map is a live link to the page it references, and that it includes as much keyword rich text as possible, enclosing the most important keywords in HTML header elements tags (e.g. h1, h2, h3). You can then use CSS to style them so they don't look awful, and … viola! you have a page that contains your target keywords within a bunch of header elements. This makes Google very, very happy.

Add an XML Sitemap

What's this, you say? Create another sitemap? You just told me to do this! Yes, we did, but the XML sitemap is a different type of sitemap for a different purpose. The one we described in the previous chapter was an HTML sitemap, designed to benefit both site visitors and search engines alike.

An XML SITEMAP is a special sitemap just for the search engines. It's different from both HTML and XHTML sitemaps. XML is a format that helps the search engines better understand the structure of your site.

Once you create your XML file, you can include it with a special meta tag so the search engines know to look at it and use it as a reference when indexing your site. Programming an XML sitemap is a bit beyond the scope of this book, so if you're not ready to tackle it, you can ask your webmaster to create one for you. On the other hand, if you are a do-it-yourself kind of website builder, there are lots of resources on the internet to help you.

If you'd like our handy guide to some of the best resources out there, drop us a line! Remember, you can find our contact information at:

www.seoannarbor.com

Use CSS for Styling

Using CSS for styling goes hand in hand with using good, clean HTML code. CSS stands for "cascading style sheets." It boils down to a way to store your **content** in a clean HTML file, and your **formatting information** in a CSS file. Why is this important?

Because using CSS makes your HTML smaller, cleaner and faster to load. And, as we've already discussed, cleaner code stands a better chance of being indexed properly by search engines.

It also makes your site easier to maintain. Let's say your site displays all H1 header tags in red with a bold font, but now you want to switch it to blue and possibly underline it. Would you rather search through the dozens of pages on your site, locating each H1 tag and manually changing the color and adding the underline, or simply editing a single entry in a CSS file and making those changes once?

Using CSS is simply a good way to clean up your site code, improve search engine rankings and make your site more maintainable. If your site isn't using CSS for styling, then you should start by asking your web designer why they are using 1990's technology. If your site hasn't been updated since the 1990's, shame on you! Otherwise shame on them!

Don't Use Deprecated Styling Tags

One of the goals of modern web design is to separate the content from the layout. As we mentioned earlier, this means you include the structure and content in the HTML file, and the formatting information in the CSS file. This keeps your code clean, allows your pages to load faster, your pages to render properly in modern browsers, and search engines to properly read and index your site.

Avoid using deprecated styling tags such as "font" or "color" in your HTML. That was an OK thing to do 15 years ago, but no longer. Those types of tags have been deprecated, meaning that they are no longer included in modern HTML specifications. Using them not only clutters your code, but also makes your site harder to maintain, and may force your site to be rendered in "quirks mode" (meaning there is no guarantee how it is going to look in any given browser).

How to Rocket Your Website to Page One of Google!

Use Keywords in Your Link Titles

You'll recall that, earlier in this book, we suggested adding ALT tags to any photos you display on your website to give the search engines an idea what the photos were about. Another way to add keywords to help guide the search engines is to use them in your link titles. By adding appropriate keywords, you let the search engines know more about the purpose and destination of each link. The "title" attribute applies to just about any HTML tag, and can be used to provide a textual description. This is especially useful for the <a href=...> ("hypertext reference") tag that's used with links on your pages. Here's how one might look:

<a title='Search Engine Optimization Ann Arbor' href='http://www.seoannarbor.com'>Search Engine Optimization Ann Arbor</a>

That link would appear to the viewer like this: **Search Engine Optimization Ann Arbor**. Clicking on it would take the viewer to: **www.seoannarbor.com**. And the search engines would have the further information supplied by the keywords in the title. By the way, when someone creates a link to your site from theirs, you should ask them to construct the links this way, too. Most webmasters, once they agree to link to you, will use the code you supply, so if you supply them with HTML that includes your desired keywords, it will boost the effect of their link to you!

Store Javascript and CSS Files Separately

Don't clutter your individual pages with embedded Javascript and CSS. Aside from being messy and harder to maintain, embedding CSS and Javascript can have an adverse effect on how quickly your page loads, and you can be penalized if your page loads too slowly (not just by search engines, but also by visitors who grow tired of waiting for your page to load). In some cases embedded CSS and Javascript code can confuse Google and the other search engines so that they can't properly index your site. If you see a bunch of stuff like this... (CSS)

```
<style type='text/css'>
body { font: 10pt verdana; background: #ffffff; text-align: center;}
.entry{
 margin-left:auto;
 margin-right: auto;
 border:1px solid black;
 width: 800px;
 text-align: left;
 padding:10px;
 min-height: 1000px;
 margin-bottom:20px;
}

h1 { font:18pt verdana; font-weight: bold; text-align: center;}
h2 { font: 16pt verdana; font-weight: bold; text-align: left; }
.right { float: right; margin-left:10px; margin-bottom:10px; }
.tip { color: red; }
</style>
```

S.E.O. and Beyond...

Or this... (Javascript)

```javascript
<script type='text/javascript'>
//ajax scripts
function createRequestObject() {
  var ro;
  var browser = navigator.appName;
  if(browser == "Microsoft Internet Explorer"){
    ro = new ActiveXObject("Microsoft.XMLHTTP");
  }else{
    ro = new XMLHttpRequest();
  }
  return ro;
}
var http = createRequestObject();
var index=-1; //used for keeping track of which item is select in a list

function sndReq(action) {
  if (http.readyState > 0 && http.readyState < 4) http.abort(); // kill if 1,2,3
  http.send(null);
  http.open('get', 'rpc.php?action='+action);
  http.onreadystatechange = handleResponse;
  http.send(null);
}
```

...mixed into your HTML code, then your site code might be considered, <ahem> cluttered. A little bit here or there might not hurt anything, but a whole bunch might!

So what's the solution? All or most of that stuff (javascript and CSS) can be included in separate files. This keeps your main website files free of clutter and easier for the search engines to understand. It makes your site faster to load since those included files can be loaded once and then cached instead being reloaded with every page request. It also makes your site easier to maintain. Sound good? We think so too. It works like this: all that messy CSS code can be stored in a separate file called "styles.css" that you'll see in the line of code below:

```
<link rel="stylesheet" href="css/styles.css" type="text/css" />
```

And all that messy Javascript code can be stored in a separate file called "custom.js."

```
<script src="js/custom.js" type="text/javascript"></script>
```

It might not always work out this way, but your goal should be to store your HTML , Javascript, and CSS code all in their own separate files.

Create an RSS Feed

The purpose of an RSS feed is to provide visitors with an automated method of seeing the latest information from your site. In other words, they can subscribe to your site and be notified of updated contents automatically. It's one more way you can include keyword rich text on your site and attract visitors.

An RSS feed is basically just an XML file that you link to within your page. Yes, it's different than an HTML or XHTML file, and yes, it IS one more thing to learn. Sorry! Here's how the line of code for the RSS feed would look:

<link rel="alternate" type='application/rss+xml' title='RSS' href='rss.php' />

If you're not sure what this means, ask your webmaster to add it for you. Or, if you're curious, a few minutes reading about RSS feeds online should help fill in some of the technical details.

Just make sure you update your site once in a while with some useful content so visitors will be more compelled to subscribe. Also, in the long run it is far easier to program an automatic RSS feed using a server side scripting language such as PHP than to manually edit the XML file every time you update your site.

Use a Server-Side Language Like PHP

Websites are written in HTML. Actually, it would be more accurate to say that web sites are rendered in HTML, as there are many server side programming languages that can be used to build your site. Two of the most popular server side languages are PHP and ASP. These languages offer many benefits, but key among them is the ability to include common files, such as a header or a footer.

This is important because pages within a site tend to have similar elements. The "header" (usually where you find the logo and main menu) is generally the same on every page, as is the bottom, where people typically include additional menu items or copyright information. If you just use HTML, you have to duplicate those common elements on every page. That's all well and good until you decide you want to change something and realize you have to go back and edit the same thing on all 25 pages of your site. No wonder people don't update their websites very often!

But if you use a server side scripting language such as PHP, you can write the header and footer once and simply include it on all subsequent pages. That way, your site will be consistent and will be much easier to update and maintain, and far more likely to be updated on a regular basis. Updating your site regularly helps attract the attention of Google. Get it? Got it. Good!

Use a Content Management System

A content management system, or CMS, is a program that allows you to easily update and manage the content on your website. A good content management system allows an average, non-technical person to update their website. Beware, however, the bad CMS, which can put up barriers between you and the code that needs to be changed as part of your ongoing SEO process. If you are an HTML guru, have a reasonably sized site, and can hack code with the best of them, then go right ahead and manually hack up your web files. The rest of us will use a CMS!

A good content management system will:

> Allow you to easily add and modify content on your site.
> Allow you to customize page titles, meta keywords and descriptions for each page.
> Allow a web designer to customize your HTML code.

A bad CMS will:

> Not allow you to customize HTML code.
> Not allow you to modify page titles and keywords.
> Be difficult to update or customize.

Section VI – WHAT MARKETING EXPERTS WANT

By now it should be clear that we think a website is meant to... communicate! And for many of us, communication means letting potential customers, clients or fans know about our idea, product or service. If you're opposed to marketing on principle, but still have an important idea to convey, we suggest you read this section anyway, because you may be able to use these suggestions to get more exposure for your ideas even if you aren't selling anything.

If you *are* trying to connect with potential fans, clients or customers, these ideas should help inspire you to modify your website in ways that can help bring more traffic, and that can turn that traffic into action. It's no coincidence, by the way, that many of these suggestions will also help your SEO – in other words, they'll help your site appear higher in search engine results while helping it become more attractive to potential customers.

Think Like a Potential Customer

One of the biggest mistakes we see people make with their websites is that they focus too much on their own point of view. Instead of putting themselves in the shoes of their potential fan, client or customer, they focus on extolling the virtues of their idea, product or service without considering what another person might actually be looking for (or *how* they'll be looking!).

> *A better approach – both for engaging users and getting more effective keywords – is to think like your potential customer. When you're creating web copy (a topic we'll talk about in other important ways in the section on social media), instead of asking, "what do I offer?" ask yourself, "What benefit am I providing my visitors?"*

Instead of creating some wacky new layout for your website that breaks all kinds of creative boundaries, spend a little time learning what people find most appealing and easiest to navigate, and use that template to construct your site. Basically, instead of having a "hey, everybody, look at me!" attitude, the key is to start with an attitude of listening. Or, as Tom Buck (one of our business mentors) likes to say: "first, seek to understand."

What Marketing Experts Want

As you'll recall from our earlier section on "What People Want," we recommend doing a bunch of keyword research to find out what web searchers are actually typing into the search engines. That's just one example of seeking to understand before you create marketing material. You may have the best cranberry infused glow-in-the-dark transparent packing tape on the planet, but if nobody's typing "cranberry infused glow-in-the-dark transparent packing tape" into Google, you may have to figure out what they're typing, and structure your web information around those topics.

It's not just about coming up with keywords. A lot of marketing gurus help work through this process by asking us to think about the difference between "features" and "benefits." A feature is an aspect of something you offer ("Our packing tape glows in the dark!"), while a benefit is the value it brings to your potential customer ("You can find our tape during those nighttime mailing runs!" or "Your reclusive sister who only comes out at night will have no problem finding your gifts in the mailbox!").

What you're trying to avoid is trumpeting all the virtues of your product and ending up with your potential customer saying, "So what?!" Instead, you want to show them how your idea, product or service will actually benefit them, hopefully prompting them to say, "That's what I've been looking for!" or "I never thought of that! Outstanding!"

S.E.O and Beyond...

On the search engine side of this process, remember this: by putting yourself in the shoes of your potential customer, you can come up with additional keywords. You've spent many years developing specialized knowledge and perfecting your skills so, as we pointed out in our What People Want section, seeing the customer's point of view can sometimes be difficult, since you already know the specialized terms that pertain to your business. There are probably a lot of people out there who don't fully understand your business, however, and that market is likely to be a lot larger than those who do.

That's the potential market for you to tap and, again, what *they're* thinking might not be what *you're* thinking.

Here's another example: an attorney who specializes in bankruptcy cases might be thinking about keywords like "bankruptcy" and "foreclosure," but his potential clients might be thinking something like, "Stop the calls!" When we researched this topic, that's a lot like what we found potential clients were actually typing into Google. The attorney got great results by optimizing his site for a key phrase similar to "stop the calls!"

So learn to think like your potential clients. What are they looking for, and how are they looking for it? Use the answers to these questions to compose web copy and to create key words and phrases to target.

Know Your USP

USP stands for "Unique Selling Proposition." This isn't strictly an SEO concept, but it can have a HUGE effect on the effectiveness of all your marketing. And when you understand your USP, you'll be able to make much better decisions about what your target audience might be.

Ask yourself, "What do we offer that's different from every other business of this type?" Your answer could be "lower prices," "better personal service," "one of a kind items," or "the best guarantee in the business." Remember, what you're looking for are those aspects of your business that are unique. Virtually every online marketplace is packed with people trying to make a buck, so you need to set yourself apart if you want to get motivated customers.

Once you know your USP, you can employ it in several different ways. First, make sure you mention it! Web visitors make instant decisions about whether to stay on your page, so tell them right away why they should stay. At our company, we say "If your website isn't on Page One of Google, contact us today!" We're lucky to have such a simple concept, but we're betting that you can identify one or two compelling benefits that you offer customers that make you unique.

How to Rocket Your Website to Page One of Google!

Remember that you should also think about your USP when you decide which keywords you want to focus on. There may be a few major keywords in your line of work that apply to everybody, but there may be a few that have a lot more relevance for people who want your particular idea, product or service.

If your focus is on quick delivery, you may be able to pair major industry keywords with words that emphasize speed. Jimmy Johns, which delivers subs, emphasizes speed ("freaky fast delivery"). If you make left handed widgets and you can fill orders within 24 hours, it makes sense to include keywords that will attract customers who want their orders filled quickly.

Finally, be sure to think about your USP in your follow up communications. If you send out emails or a newsletter, construct your stories or advertisements to support your USP. If your USP is all about low price, you'd be working against yourself if you sent out an ad promoting high quality, expensive products. If your USP is all about speed of delivery, you should think twice about an offer for a custom manufactured product that takes two months to ship.

Include a Call to Action

Make sure you you include a promiment and compelling call to action on your site! A call to action is a noticeable link or button that encourages the visitor to "click here to learn more", "get started today," or "buy now." Basically, you want a big, noticeable link that makes it really easy and really obvious for visitors to purchase your products or services, subscribe to your newsletter, or whatever else it is you'd like them to do.

You'll almost never go broke by making things on your website simple enough for a four year-old. Our statistics show that people leave sites in a big hurry when they have trouble figuring out what action to take. You don't want to do all of the work to promote and optimize your site only to have visitors leave without making a purchase or contacting you for a quote. Give them every opportunity by including a call to action.

Speaking of calls to action, don't forget that you can get our guide to what the young folks call a "crap-ton" of web design, coding, marketing, and SEO resources absolutely free. You can get it by contacting us. Remember, our website is located at:

www.seoannarbor.com

S.E.O. and Beyond...

Write for the Web

Web readers don't read the same way people read books! If you're over 30 or if you're academically inclined, this can be one of the hardest lessons to learn, but one of the most important. People tend to read books in the order the words are presented ... starting at the top and reading every line until the end of the page. Web readers DO NOT read this way, and if you write "bookish" text for your website, you do so at your own peril.

Web readers scan. They look at certain parts of the page first, and skip around the page looking for content, images, or links that are useful to them. We discussed how to lay out your pages earlier in this book, but when it comes to presenting text, here's how you should organize it: header, text, header, text, header, text ... and throw in useful links here and there as well!

Your headers should be short and they should contain a summary of the paragraph that follows them. Make sure your headers are clearly set apart from the other text so viewers can locate and scan them easily. Whenever possible, say something compelling. Make your best points, exaggerate slightly, be funny, or distort a common catch phrase to get people's attention. If they're interested in your topic, they'll scan to that header and follow up by scanning the text.

What Marketing Experts Want

But even in the paragraph following the headers, avoid going on at length. Make your points quickly and clearly. We can't emphasize enough that web readers are impatient. They're used to getting what they want quickly, so you better give it to them. If you absolutely must explain something in great detail, provide a link at the end of a short intro paragraph that takes your most interested readers to another page or pages where you can expound to your heart's content. Just remember to include lots of keywords in your lengthy PhD thesis so you get the SEO boost you need from all that text!

Under Promise and Over Deliver

We realize this is one of the most hackneyed phrases in all of salesdom, but there's still a hefty dose of truth in the idea that failing to deliver on your promises can hurt you in the long run. As we mentioned earlier, great marketing can cause a bad business to fail even faster than it would fail without any marketing at all, because it can get a lot more people to try your business. If a lot of people have a bad experience with you, they'll talk about it.

So make it a point to know what you're good at and exactly how you can help potential visitors to your site. Tell them what you do in compelling terms, but don't promise them the moon unless you can absolutely deliver it, wrapped in tissue paper and tied to their chimney. If there are one or two things you like to do for your favorite customers that goes above and beyond what they expect, consider saving those things and maybe not trumpeting them from the figurative rooftops of your website.

And as we hope we've made clear, when you do get motivated people to enlist in your sales process, treat them well. Making the world a better place lies at the heart of the most successful businesses, and you'll get incredibly loyal followers if you truly help them.

Include Keyword-Related Questions

Another technique for attracting visitors to your site is to consider the problems your ideas, products or services solve, and pose those problems as questions for your visitors. In other words – how can you help *them*? If you're an SEO company, your goal is to help clients improve their search engine rankings and ultimately get them to the very top of Page One. You can create visitor interest by framing that idea like this: "Help! My site isn't showing up in Google!" Or: "How do I get my website to the top of Google?"

But that's not all. Think about why your customers want to be listed prominently in search engines. To be above the competition? To attract more visitors? To increase business? Turn those goals into statements or questions that lead your visitors to understand that you can help achieve them. We'll talk more about this thinking process in our section on Social Media.

At this point you can probably understand why this is compelling for visitors. You may be asking yourself, however, how this helps with SEO. Here's how: first, it provides you with yet another opportunity to include keyword-rich text on your site. That's a Bonus. Second, by thinking about the problems you help your customers solve, you're likely to come up with additional keywords, which can then be included in your content. Double bonus!

Offer Free Stuff

The entire marketing world has come to realize the high value of contact information for people who are interested in what you provide. Make sure you capture and retain information about your visitors. Here's a helpful way to get it: in a prominent place on your site (like the upper right corner of every page), include an "opt-in" bar - a place where visitors can provide their email in return for some kind of free perk you provide automatically.

The technical aspects of this may be slightly beyond most do it yourself web builders, but many graphical web building tools provide a ready made email bar or link to send an email. If your sales volume is low, you can manually save emails to a file. If you do a lot of business, however, we recommend automating this even if you have to pay an expert a few bucks to build the feature for you.

Be sure to keep it simple. We've learned on the streets of experience that asking for too much information can kill a lot of interest. Just ask for an email - the really interested visitors will give you a real email and they'll follow up if the perk you offer is compelling. What you give them in return for their email depends on the nature of your business. If you're in retail, you could provide a discount coupon. If you're a consultant, you could provide an article or how-to that helps visitors with a niche aspect of your business. If you provide some kind of instruction, you could send out a mini-lesson on video.

Unless you like being really busy, we recommend not only using an automated system for capturing and storing the emails, but also an automated system for sending out the thing you're giving them. That's why we like coupons, articles, and videos. They can be delivered digitally, so there's no shipping costs or any need for employee time spent responding to emails. And if your webmaster can link the email capture to your digital newsletter (like Constant Contact or some similar system), your interested visitors will automatically be included in your client recruiting process.

The whole point of SEO is to attract more people to your site who otherwise might not go there, or who might visit your competitors. And once they get to your site, you want to enlist them in some way in your idea, product or service. Let's face it, not everyone is going to buy from you, at least not right away. But they might be willing to at some point in the future, especially if you've become a trusted advisor.

We'll talk a lot more about this in our section on Social Media!

How to Rocket Your Website to Page One of Google!

Use Checklists for Engagement

Another way to engage readers attention is to use checklists. With basic programming skills or decent web design software, you can make the checklists interactive. You could offer a list of problems your potential customer might experience. Here's an example:

> [ ] My website doesn't get enough traffic!
> [ ] Visitors come to my website, but nobody buys!
> [ ] I get lots of calls, but not from clients I want!
> [ ] I can't my webmaster to return my calls!
> [ ] I don't have a website for my business, but I want one!

You could set up the checklist so that if viewers check a minimum number of entries, they are automatically directed to a page with information tailored to their concerns. Or, if automated websites don't appeal to you, you could just end with a prompt for the visitor's email, and follow up manually.

Like our other strategies, this one works on more than one level. It increases visitor interaction with the site, keeping them interested and keeping them on your page longer. It gives you information about visitors that you wouldn't otherwise get. If you automate it, you can provide intelligent responses to increase their sense of involvement without having to do any work in person.

Add Smiling Faces

Whatever else you do to make sure people find your website, make sure they're happy and interested when they get there. The most important thing you can do, of course, is make sure to offer compelling, relevant content. A close second, however, is to include high quality photographs of smiling people.

Ask yourself how the mood of your webpage is established. Besides the words on the page, the layout, color scheme, and photographs are critical. If you're not sure which of those three aspects is most important, find a webpage that has very little color and a very prominent photograph. The photo is a gazillion times more important to creating the initial impression than any other element! Our research shows that people respond most positively to photos of other smiling, happy people, engaged in activities that relate to the subject matter of the website.

If you have the budget, we recommend hiring a professional photographer who's experienced in shooting photos for the web. If you have a limited budget, you can buy photos from sites that offer royalty free photos, like iStockPhoto, 123rf.com, or shutterstock.com. Keep in mind, however, that "royalty free" doesn't mean "free"! You still have to open an account and pay a licensing fee.

S.E.O. and Beyond...

Add Cute Animals

This is a variation on our previous tip, in which we suggested including photos of smiling faces on your site. If the content is appropriate, include photos of cute animals. If you haven't studied the way people interact with content on the web, you might be surprised at how motivated people are to share cute animal pictures. There's a gut level reaction to attractive images that causes web viewers to take action, and it's critical to leverage their emotions if you want to make an impact on the internet.

As we've hinted at elsewhere in this book, you don't want to fill your website with *only* cute images while neglecting to include the content your viewers really want, unless your site is somehow related directly to the idea of cute images. But creating that "blink" moment when a visitor forms his or her instantaneous impression of the worth of your site is one of the most important things you can do to brand your product or business. Great examples of this are things like Tony the Tiger (Frosted Flakes), the Gekko (Geico), and the Pillsbury Dough Boy. Nearly everybody knows what products these mascots represent, and virtually everybody in the target audience has a good impression of them.

Our research shows that people respond positively to photos of cute animals almost without regard to the subject matter of the website!

By the way, if you're looking for an animal mascot, there are a surprising number of cheap places to have one drawn up. One place we've gone to get a variety of different takes on a design idea like a mascot or a logo is fiverr.com, where you can get almost any imaginable web task done for $5.00. You won't get high quality work at that price point, but you can give a handful of people the same task and get a portfolio of initial ideas to focus your thinking. If we find a designer at fiverr.com who creates an image we like, we'll ask him or her to take the design to the next level. If not, we'll give our top few choices to one of the local designers we work with and let that person work up the final images.

How to Rocket Your Website to Page One of Google!

Add a Pretty Girl

This will probably be our most controversial suggestion on how to amp up the visual impact of your website: add a photo of a pretty girl.

The fact that people respond to images of attractive women will surprise nobody except those who've been living in a cave for the last 100 years. The truth is, an attractive person of either gender will work, and if you're offering something like massages by handsome men, the images probably ought to be male rather than female. We're NOT suggesting that you post lacivious or pornographic images on your website, so please don't write to complain that we're telling you to become a smut peddler! There's enough of that sort of thing on the internet already ... or so people tell us.

Instead, what we're suggesting is that you employ attractive images on your pages whenever it's appropriate, and that for most endeavors involving humans, photos of people who are nice to look at, engaged in activity that relates to your idea, product or service, will have the most positive impact.

And whatever you do, don't just simply steal photos from other websites. It's not just unethical, it's also illegal, and sooner or later, somebody always seems to discover when we .... er, you ... "borrow" a photo without permission!

Include a Page of Misspellings

When you did your keyword research in the first section of this book, you may have found that misspellings of your idea, product or service appeared in the top 100 most searched keywords. We find this a lot, so before you say, "I would never want any misspelled words on my website," think about this: even people who can't spell have credit cards. So snub them at your own peril! Instead, it makes sense to find ways to appeal to those who are clumsy on the keyboard, just in case they're folks who might be interested in what you offer. One way is to include a page of misspellings, or if a page is too much for your taste, just an inset box somewhere on a page dealing with your offerings.

This provides content for the search engines so when people accidentally type "wijjets" instead of "widgets," your page will appear in the search results. However, if you really want to leverage this concept, find a way to make the page appeal to humans as well as robots. You could make the content funny or informative, and make sure you use your page titles to let people know there's funny content, something like this:

> Hilarious Misspellings of Common Martial Arts Terms
> How a Redneck Might Spell Military Words
> I Hate my Phone's Auto-Correct!

S.E.O. and Beyond...

Participate in or Host a Forum

Participate in a forum related to your idea, product or service. Better still, host one of your own. There is a huge array of platforms that allow you to host a forum. This gives you the opportunity to create a meeting place for people interested in the same subjects as you. Once you've amassed a following of people who regularly visit and post comments, you've got a built-in place to find out about current opinions, to advertise, to pursuade, to create controversy, or to become a noted authority on your topic.

Be forewarned, however, that getting a forum to the point where it's popular can be a huge amount of work. For that reason, we don't recommend that you start from scratch unless the forum is your primary website and you plan to do all the things we recommend in this book to promote it.

Instead, enlist a few very vocal followers and build an audience by allowing comments on a page of your site or on your blog. As you get comfortable with the process of moderating the comments and encouraging participation, gradually build your audience. At some point, it will make sense to have a dedicated place where they can go opine, argue, and ask for help. If you're the host, that gives you a lot of control over what visitors see when they come to chat. That, friends, can be a very powerful marketing tool!

Create an FAQ List

F.A.Q. stands for "frequently asked questions." At one point this concept was almost revolutionary in its power to attract visitors. However, we've tracked responses to FAQ pages and found that people are gradually growing immune to their appeal. Yet there's still a place for FAQ's because their benefits work on several levels.

The most obvious way FAQ's work is by attracting people who want quick answers and who don't feel like reading your whole site to find them. They see a link to the FAQ page on your home page, click it, then quickly scroll down to see if their concern is addressed.

A second way in which FAQ pages help is that they allow you to add a ton of keywords and phrases to your page. You mention your keywords again and again without having to simply list them or otherwise create some artificial excuse for them to appear. This helps, as do most of our tips, with the search engine robots.

A third way FAQ's can help is that they can allow you to influence the thinking of your visitors. If you pose questions that relate to your USP (the "unique selling proposition" that we mentioned earlier), you get visitors thinking about that rather than about some other aspect of the topic. If the answers showcase the virtues of what you do, they may be more likely to do business with you.

Include a Top Ten List

As we explained earlier, the benefits of keyword gimmicks like FAQ's are gradually losing their persuasive power among your human visitors. Top ten lists are in the same boat - they're not as effective as they used to be, but they're still worth including.

Just like FAQ's, top ten lists tend to attract people who are looking for quick answers and want to find them without having to do a lot of searching. Just the idea of a top ten list suggests the most important facts around your idea, product or service, and that they won't be forced to read a lot of content to learn those facts. Also like FAQ's, top ten lists allow you add keywords in every item on the list without it seeming like an articifical list you included solely for the purpose of packing more keywords on your pages.

You can tailor your top ten list to reflect your particular speciality. If you say, "whatever you do, make sure your left handed widget provider supplies you with these ten key services," and you just happen to provide those services, that's a benefit to you. Further, if those ten key pieces are also justifiably the most important things someone seeking your idea, product or service should know, then you're doing a real service to visitors. Helping the world become a better place by improving your website's search engine placement is pretty darn rewarding, if you ask us!

Include Funny Stuff ... and Say So!

If you include humor or attention-getting content, you're more likely to get visitors who might not otherwise visit. A corollary to this suggestion is that you should also let your visitors know there's funny stuff to be found. Humor, when handled well, creates engagement and shareability. We'll talk more about these concepts in our section on Social Media, but for now, the key is to understand that people on the internet like to be entertained, and they share things that entertain them. If people seek out your website because of humor, more eyes will see your content. If they let others know they found funny stuff on your site, the others will visit, and some of the others will share. You'll have more traffic and more links to your site floating around on the internet, in such places as emails, Twitter, Facebook, Pinterest, and LinkedIn.

To understand the value of saying, "hey, this is funny," on your humorous page or Youtube video, think about how people share stuff on the web. They often paste a link into their preferred social media platform. If those links contain a snippet that reads, "hey, this is funny," people who might not want to be bothered with serious content might click on the link just to be entertained. They come, they laugh, they share, and ... they just might buy, or share with someone else who will!

Include Videos on Your Home Page

Videos are great for numerous reasons. Most people spend more time watching TV than they do reading or listening to the radio, and a lot of web users watch video rather than read content. Also, a short video can often be used to explain or introduce something that would require a quite a lot of reading. Just make sure you also include a text explanation containing the relevant keywords since text works for SEO purposes, and video doesn't.

Posting a video to YouTube will expose you to a far wider potential audience than simply posting it on your website. If you post something on your site, only visitors who already come to your site will see it. When you post something on YouTube, there is a greater chance that some of the millions of YouTube viewers will see it.

Also, linking from your YouTube account to your website gets you another "free" link, while increasing the chances that a motivated viewer will actually come to the site just because of the content in the video. And finally, if you embed the YouTube videos on your home page or another relevant page of your website, and add new videos regularly, the slight change in your site will be noted by Google. Updates help convince Google that something's going on (rather than the site being absolutely the same for months at a time) and they'll give you a little credit for the update.

Include Tutorials

People are very likely to be either shopping or learning when they use the web. We've talked more than a bit about how important content is, both to Google and to your human visitors, and tutorials are a great way to increase the relevance of your site to people who want to learn about your idea, product or service. If they're not ready to buy, a strong sales message will probably send them elsewhere, so if you have some pages dedicated to help those in the learning stage, you're far more likely to retain them.

Well written tutorials, first and foremost, teach visitors about your topic. Secondly, they allow you to include more keywords on your pages. Thirdly, they help build trust for your brand. And fourth, if they're crafted with an eye toward your particular specialty, they'll help those who eventually decide to become buyers rather than learners to buy from you rather than from someone else.

Incentivize Your Visitors

You may have noticed that access to information is no longer the barrier that separates the provider from the seeker. A motivated person can learn almost all there is to know about a topic, given enough time and an average understanding of how to search the web. What you need to do to stand out is to make sure the information you provide is organized in such a way as to make it more convenient, more entertaining, or more useful. And you need to show those qualities very quickly. One way to do so is to offer incentives.

An incentive could be a handy, printable how-to guide. It could be a product sample. It could be a discount coupon. It could be a video available only to subscribers. As you'll see in the next section, your portfolio of incentives should probably consist of all these things, organized in such a way as to attract people and to keep them interested, preferably getting them more and more motivated the longer they're around. If you're actually concerned about being an asset to humanity rather than just another salesperson, the incentives should provide real value for your fellow human beings.

Incentivize visitors to your social media to come to your website. Incentivize your website visitors to enlist in your newsletter. Incentivize your subscribers to urge others to visit your site. Incentivize people to comment on your blog, videos and Facebook posts.

Section VII – SOCIAL MEDIA

*We're using the words "social," "social sharing," and "social media" a bit differently than most other experts. In this book, those words refer to virtually any activity you do that helps increase your visibility in your market niche that also has a footprint outside your website and is interconnected across different platforms. It's **social** because it engages both human and robot eyeballs, and because it's part of an ecosystem of information, links, and interactions.*

Handle with care! When executed properly, this form of intensely focused, multi-platform social campaign can revolutionize your business.

S.E.O. and Beyond...

Getting seen on the internet is much, much harder than it was just a decade ago. When the world wide web first came into existence, it was enough just to have a simple website. People would find you. As the number of websites grew, however, your site would be overlooked unless it had unique or especially useful information. Then, beginning around ten years ago, it became necessary to do at least some SEO work if you wanted more than a few visitors. A little social media was also helpful to increase interest in your idea, product or service, but not necessarily required.

Today, however, an occasional witty comment on Facebook is no longer enough. Those who truly want to be noticed must engage in a robust, consistent, well-thought-out awareness campaign for each niche they want to occupy.

In this section, we'll talk about our MAGNIFICENT SEVEN of awareness building: Twitter, Facebook, Blogs, Youtube, LinkedIn, articles, and an email newsletter. More importantly, we'll get you thinking about how to use them to maximize the impact of your work. The world of Social Media (the way we define it) is evolving fast, so it's critical not to rely too much on a single platform, but to always be efficient, tactical and widespread.

Now, let's get to it before somebody invents the next FaceBlog-Toogle and changes how we do marketing on the web yet again!

Social Media

Utilize the "Magnificent Seven" Platforms

As we just mentioned, for a complete social media strategy, you should have an understanding of how to use Twitter, Facebook, Blogs, Youtube, LinkedIn, articles and an email newsletter. There are many other sharing platforms out there, of course. If your idea, product or service is suited to a specific platform, you should get very familiar with it and use it consistently. For example, Pinterest comes to mind as a place where retailers can post images of their products and visitors can post those images to their own collections. If you're a retailer of products that work with the type of audience Pinterest attracts, you owe it to yourself to do a little research on that platform.

Most of us who have websites to promote, however, should make sure we have some combination of the MAGNIFICENT SEVEN under control before taking on more specific forms of social sharing. Each platform has a slightly different purpose, and all not only boost your presence outside your website, they can also encourage motivated visitors to come to your website or to another platform where you can help educate them about your subject area.

We'll talk more fully about how to make sure you're using each platform to its fullest potential in the next chapter, but first, here's a quick and dirty explanation of each platform.

How to Rocket Your Website to Page One of Google!

Twitter

Twitter is a "micro-blogging" service that lets you send out messages of up to 140 characters. Those messages can be received on computers, smart phones, and even on some simple flip phones. Twitter is currently one of the ten most-visited sites on the internet!

Facebook

At the moment, Facebook is the king of social platforms on the web, boasting over one billion active users. You can share photos, videos, links to internet content, status updates, events, comments, and more. You can create a page for your company or a group of like-minded people.

Blogs

Blogs are sites that allow you to post information such as text, photos and videos. Typically, visitors to a blog expect to see content written by a single author or a small group of authors, with the posts displayed in reverse chronological order. Visitors can comment on the posts. Blogger is currently the most widely used platform, with Wordpress running a close second.

Youtube

On Youtube, you can post videos along with a limited amount of text and links. You can create your own Youtube channel, and also share posted videos on your website, your blog, in your Facebook feed, and by including links in your articles and newsletters.

LinkedIn

LinkedIn is a social networking site originally designed for professionals. You can post a profile, your resume, photos, and various other content, as well as send messages to your contacts. LinkedIn says it has over 200 million active users.

Articles

Articles are not normally thought of as social or sharing platforms, but we included them because they share many of the most important features of the other five platforms: they can work both within and outside your website, they provide content, they can include links or videos, they can be shared, and they can be separated into smaller parts and leveraged across the other platforms.

Newsletters

Mail Chimp, iContact, and Constant Contact are all utilities that can help you create and send newsletters and manage your audience. You can do almost anything in a newsletter than you can do in your website or in any of the other social media, but because it should be sent to people who have already expressed an interest in your idea, product or service, you can tailor the content a bit more, and leverage the fact that your readers will be slightly more motivated than the average accidental visitor.

Now, on to what is probably one of the most important chapters in this book: Use Powerful Social Media Strategies.

S.E.O. and Beyond...

Use Powerful Social Media Strategies

Each platform we've mentioned works in a slightly different way. Your mission is to develop a grand strategy to promote your idea, product or service, and apply it across all the platforms. Those who simply open a Twitter account and just post random thoughts are doomed to internet mediocrity. Knowledge and planning are power in any endeavor, and internet visibility is no exception. Here are the SIX ESSENTIALS of a well-crafted social strategy:

1. A narrowly tailored message.
2. Engaging content.
3. Keywords and phrases to emphasize your message.
4. Links.
5. One campaign across all platforms.
6. Best practices.

A Narrowly Tailored Message

Narrowly tailor your message to appeal to your target audience. If you sell pink left handed widgets and your largest customer segment is divorced women over 40, then simply advertising "widgets!" to everybody on the internet is a waste of your advertising time, effort and money. Figure out what kinds of conversations these women are having and where they're having them, and get involved by offering something useful about the topics they're already interested in.

Social Media

There's almost no limit to how far you should go to identify the specific people who are likely to be your best customers. Some factors to consider are: gender, age, location, economic status, hobbies, careers, marital status, travel habits, subscription choices, medical history, clubs, vehicle choice, social or political causes, number and gender of children, favorite movies or books, and on and on. Get to know them intimately (without stalking anybody!) and figure out exactly what they want. Then construct the topic or theme for your campaign.

To help you understand how this might look, let's run with the deeply fascinating concept of pink left-handed widgets and divorced women over 40. Suppose your research shows that these women are interacting about widgets over Facebook, and they're talking about trips to Las Vegas for pink left-handed widget conventions. Also suppose that a lot of purchases at your online store happen just before, during, and just after these conventions.

On Facebook, you'd get involved in the groups that plan and share news about the conventions. You'd want to tweet ideas about the new versions of pink widgets coming out at convention time. On your blog, you could share trip planning ideas, give discounts, or talk about your adventures in Las Vegas. On Youtube, you could show a tour of the venue, or find customers to do product reviews. On LinkedIn, you could start your own group of convention attendees or link with other providers of pink left-handed widgets.

You could write articles about planning for the convention trips or reviewing the experience, either to post on your website or in other places that allow you to share content. And you could re-purpose any or all of the information we just mentioned to use in your email newsletter. We'll pick up a similar story a bit later, but keep in mind for now that once you've chosen your NARROWLY TAILORED MESSAGE, you're going to try to find ways to apply it across all your platforms.

Engaging Content

Include content that makes viewers want to engage with you. If you've done your homework in figuring out exactly who your target customers are and what they're interested in, the topics to include in your content will become very clear. That's half the battle in making sure your social media is interesting to your visitors. To fully understand what it means to be "engaging," however, we've broken the concept into two parts: engaging1 and engaging2.

Engaging 1

Engaging1 means making sure your NARROWLY TAILORED MESSAGE is interesting to your potential visitors or customers. If you did your homework properly when creating that message, it should be inherently interesting to them, because you've built it around topics and platforms where they're already involved. If you want to amp up the interest level, and have a real impact on your visitors, combine the NARROWLY TAILORED MESSAGE with something that raises their emotional involvement. Here's a list of ways to make the message even more engaging1 to your visitors: use humor, inspiration, how-to, touching emotion, incentives (like free videos, articles, gift cards, pens, advice, etc.), beauty, education, buying tips, "top secret" stuff, surprises, babies, insider info, a good cause, sarcasm, gaming hacks, celebrities, good looking animals, hot women or men, politics, or sex.

Engaging2

The other half the battle of engagement is in how you present the information. When we say "engaging2," we mean more than "interesting." We mean that your visitors will engage with you by offering their contact information, sharing your posts, commenting on your posts, clicking on your links, or otherwise taking some action that increases your knowledge of them, increases others' knowledge of you, or increases your knowledge of others. This is such an important point we're going to say it again in big, bold letters:

ENGAGEMENT2 MEANS YOUR VISITORS TAKE SOME ACTION THAT INCREASES YOUR KNOWLEDGE OF THEM, INCREASES OTHERS' KNOWLEDGE OF YOU, OR INCREASES YOUR KNOWLEDGE OF OTHERS!

Here's a list of some of the possible actions a visitor could take that increases your knowledge of them: they take a survey, supply their email in return for some kind of perk, answer a direct question, accept a newsletter subscription, click on a link, ask a question, use a coupon, comment on a post, "like" a Facebook page, and so on.

Here's a list of some of the possible ways a visitor could take action that increases *others'* knowledge of *you*: they share a Facebook post, repost a video, email their friends about you, share a coupon, comment or ask a question, invite their friends to an event, talk about you in social media, talk about you on review or rating sites, review your idea, product or service on Google Places, post a sticker, flyer, or decal, give away a pen or other brand perk, etc.

And here's a list of some of the possible ways a visitor could increase *your* knowledge of *others*: they could answer a survey, give you a direct referral, suggest your page to friends, bring a friend to your business or event, recommend a friend to you on LinkedIn, recruit you to help out at a social or cause-related group, put two businesses together for a joint project, etc.

So, the question you should ask when you're developing your campaign is something like this: within my NARROWLY TAILORED MESSAGE, what approach should I take that would encourage my visitors to take one or more of the engagement2 actions? This is the second really important point we've made in just a few pages, so here come the bold letters again…

WHAT APPROACH SHOULD I TAKE TO ENCOURAGE MY VISITORS TO TAKE ONE OR MORE ENGAGEMENT2 ACTIONS?

Answer that question and you'll be well on your way to using social media and sharing to the fullest extent possible!

Keywords and Phrases to Emphasize your Message

Use keywords and phrases that emphasize your message. The more specific these phrases are, the better. If your topic or theme is "Hawaiian vacations for thirty-something couples with no children," then you'll want to brainstorm a list of potential keywords that might look something like this:

> hawaii
> vacation
> couples resorts
> kid-free resorts
> couples in their thirties
> the anniversary getaway

... and so forth. For a campaign, you'll want to research these terms the way we suggested near the beginning of this book, using the Adwords keyword tool or whatever tool you find is most helpful. The goal is to come up with a single, highly-focused key phrase that encapsulates the niche you want to reach. It might be something like this: "kid-free resorts in Hawaii for my anniversary vacation." That phrase then becomes the seed you plant to grow content for each of the MAGNIFICENT SEVEN social platforms.

Tweet it on Twitter. Post it on Facebook. Include it in a paragraph on your blog or on LinkedIn. Make it the title of an article you add to your website and submit it to a site that features information about kid-free travel. Use it as the anchor text in your links.

Links

Use links in all possible ways to ensure that both your human visitors and the search engine robots know exactly what niche you're in. The most obvious place to point your links is to the home page on your website, but that's not always the best place to send people. Instead, these links should point to the place you want your potential customers to go to get them engaged, in both the engagement1 and engagement2 sense of the word.

For example, if you have some really excellent information pertaining to your key phrase on a blog post or in an article page on your website, you could send them there, especially if that content is crafted in such as way as to motivate visitors to comment, share, or subscribe to your newsletter. Once visitors have become part of your dialogue, you can provide them with very valuable or useful information, so that they start to think of you as a resource whenever the topic crosses their mind.

Keep in mind that Twitter is short and potentially the most frequent, Facebook and LinkedIn are typically longer and less frequent, Blog posts a bit longer, and articles longest of all and the most static.

One way to approach the use of links is to use them to "promote" your visitors to the next longer form of media, being sure to offer value at every step of the way. Here's an example:

Twitter: Post "I fell in love again on my anniversary vacation in Hawaii!" Provide a link to your Facebook page.

Facebook: Post a video of a couple talking about how they fell in love again in Hawaii, emphasizing the benefits of the couples-only resort, and mentioning how helpful your blog was in suggesting activities and providing discounts. Provide a link to your blog.

Blog: Include two paragraphs on the wonderful anniversary vacation you had in Hawaii, what you did, and how you saved money. Provide a link to an article page where than can find complete information, or suggest that they sign up for your newsletter.

Article: On your website, post a complete article (rather than just two paragraphs) on your Hawaiian vacation, with an opt-in utility where visitors can get a detailed list of resources and ideas in return for providing their email address.

Newsletter: Once you have the email address of potential customers, make sure you don't abuse it. Newsletters should be delivered only to those who have opted in, so links in your newsletter serve a slightly different purpose when it comes to your human visitors. Provide them with truly useful information at tasteful intervals (once a week is probably the limit of frequency for most newsletters – less often is usually better), and make sure you give far more than you ask. They're already involved in your engagement process, so you should make sure you're giving them value to keep them engaged, and only selling to them or "promoting" them to more profitable customers when it makes sense. We think offering something useful at least three times for every time you ask for a sale or an action is about the minimum ratio.

One Campaign Across All Platforms

Make sure your message is consistent across all the MAGNIFICENT SEVEN platforms. As we pointed out in the last chapter, each level of social media should provide value or interest, and at the same time should be useful enough to encourage some of your visitors to go to the next larger platform or to opt in to your newsletter.

If you employ a different message or theme in the different platforms, you lose the benefit of having visitors get involved in learning more and getting more committed to you as a resource. And, almost as important, you lose the effect of having a bunch of links associated with the exact same keywords across all the platforms (which is meant to give all your platforms a boost in the eyes of the search engine robots).

This approach also increases your efficiency. As you've probably gathered by now, developing your NARROWLY TAILORED MESSAGE, creating marketing materials, making sure they appear across all the MAGNIFICENT SEVEN platforms, and making sure you've got useful links everywhere is a LOT of work!

But at least if you make sure you're focusing on one campaign across all the platforms, you can repurpose your materials for each platform without having to write everything from scratch for each one. We'll talk a bit more about that in the next chapter, so for now, let's move on to the last of the SIX ESSENTIALS of a well-crafted internet marketing campaign.

Best Practices

Use best practices for each platform according to its character. We've already touched on this, but a 140 character post on Twitter is going to have a different look and feel than a five paragraph article on ArticleCity.com, and it's going to serve a different purpose. Take a little time to understand each platform and how best to use it, and the effectiveness of your efforts will be increased exponentially. Keep in mind, too, that almost everything on the internet is changing rapidly, so it's important to keep up with the evolution of specific technologies and to understand what "best practices" means for Social Media in a general sense. The overview below is so important we'll repeat it again at the end of this chapter:

> *Give more than you ask. Across all your Social Media platforms, provide information of real value within your NARROWLY TAILORED MESSAGE. Make it engaging in* **both** *senses of the word. If you're trying to drive traffic to your website or to your other platforms, provide a link and make it clear why it's beneficial for visitors to click on the link. That could mean they'll find useful information at the destination, or it could mean they'll get an incentive. Test and measure. If something's not working, improve it. If it's still not working, remove it. Be relentless. Never, ever, ever give up.*

Twitter: for Twitter, the golden rule is that you should listen more than you Tweet. Take the time to find conversations within your NARROWLY TAILORED MESSAGE and do your research before Tweeting. What are people already talking about? What Tweets get the best responses? What sort of Tweets seem to create hostility or derision? Track the trends within your NARROWLY TAILORED MESSAGE, and see where the conversations tend to go.

Once you know what you want to Tweet about, and how to Tweet about it, make sure you're genuine and don't come across as too pushy or sales-y. If you do well, you'll build credibility over time, and you don't want to mortgage that credibility by pushing too hard. If you're marketing a business, we recommend that you use a company-branded Twitter account rather than your personal account. And finally, be consistent. Post regularly without extensive time lapses, and keep the tone of your Tweets consistent with your brand and your NARROWLY TAILORED MESSAGE.

Facebook: For Facebook, the posts are longer (and you can include photos or videos), but the etiquette is similar to Twitter. It's not that you can't post anything you want, it's just that people's reactions make a lot more difference when you're building a company brand than when you're catching up with your friends. Find Facebook groups or company pages that relate to your idea, product or service, and pay attention to the kinds of information that get the most positive responses. When it makes sense, LIKE the most popular of those pages and interact with them.

And be consistent! Just as with Twitter, post regularly without extensive time lapses between posts, and keep the tone of your posts consistent with your brand and your NARROWLY TAILORED MESSAGE. Make your social activities a priority:

> Build it into your schedule.
> Make it a habit.
> Keep it short - you don't need to write War and Peace every week.

S.E.O. and Beyond...

> Talk about new products.
> Talk about sales and promotions.
> Talk about events.
> Talk about your best customers.
> Repurpose the articles and keyword text you've written according to our previous suggestions.
> Just do it!

Blogs: blog posts can be longer than Facebook posts. They can even be complete articles if your writing is compelling enough to keep your audience involved for several paragraphs. The keys are to make sure you're writing within the confines of your NARROWLY TAILORED MESSAGE, that you're thinking about both engagement1 and engagement2, and that you know exactly what you're trying to accomplish with your post.

It's not that you can't ever just post something you find interesting or amusing, but it's critical to remember that hitting home runs in Social Media can be a lot of work, and if you spend your precious time posting without a purpose, you may find you don't have enough time to craft your purpose-driven posts.

Youtube: videos are one of the areas where we find that people easily fall off track. They either want to try to produce something so incredible that it threatens to consume their entire marketing

ing budget, or they pay so little attention to the visual impact of their scenes that they ignore things that would really turn off their potential visitors. You can scale your production values according to the size of the market you're in ... unless you're Coca-Cola or Nike, you probably don't need your videos to look like they were produced by Steven Spielberg. And whatever you do, don't stray from your NARROWLY TAILORED MESSAGE. YouTube, like the other platforms in our MAGNIFICENT SEVEN, is just another component in your complete internet marketing campaign.

LinkedIn: LinkedIn is slightly less "social" than Facebook and Twitter, in the sense that users tend to update less frequently, and because of the business orientation, they tend to focus on more serious updates. But there are still a lot of opportunities to feature your ideas, products and services on LinkedIn, including on your profile under "Experience," or "Publications," and on your updates.

To help figure out the best ways to make your presence known on LinkedIn, take the time to find updates or groups within your NARROWLY TAILORED MESSAGE. What are the people in those groups talking about? What updates get the best response? Do some updates seem to fall on deaf ears or attract a lot of negative comments? Pay attention to who's getting the most traction within your NARROWLY TAILORED MESSAGE, and use their approach as a launching pad when building your own presence on LinkedIn.

How to Rocket Your Website to Page One of Google!

Just don't forget what we said back in the chapter about articles in our What Robots Want section. People don't read web content the same way as they read books or printed matter. They scan quickly, looking for keywords or phrases that interest them, and most only settle down to read a paragraph after they've located the sub-topic that's most important to them. As we pointed out, for your articles it's best to include frequent headers, set apart from your paragraphs of text, that clearly indicate exactly what each paragraph is about. And don't go on forever … get to the point quickly!

Email Newsletters: the biggest differences between email newsletters and the other MAGNIFICENT SEVEN platforms is that your readers have already opted in or have otherwise shown interest in your idea, product or service. So instead of being a platform with which you're trying to get them to enlist with you, a newsletter is a platform with which you are trying to continue to provide value, and hopefully increase your subscribers' trust in you over time. For that reason, you sometimes have to exceed your comfort zone by giving information that's very valuable.

Remember, in most places with internet access, especially in North America, there are many others who can offer visitors some alternative to your idea, product or service. If you alienate your subscribers, give them inaccurate information, or simply bore them, they'll likely unsubscribe. If you already have a newsletter, you can

Social Media

bet that a number of your subscribers read the information your competitors distribute in addition to yours. Every time you communicate, you're either more interesting or less interesting, more valuable or less valuable than your competitors. Your future best client could already be engaged in your enlistment process but just not ready to buy or further interact with you today. So make sure that when they do become ready to spend money or take the action you want them to take, they think of you as someone they can trust, someone who provides incredible value. Let their thought process be this one:

> *"I've been following Business A and Business B for months. They both seem to know what they're doing, but every time I get Business A's newsletter, I learn something useful. If they're this good when I'm not even spending any money with them, I can only imagine what kind of value they'll provide when I'm actually their customer!"*

So we've come to the end of this chapter on best practices. As promised, on the next page we'll repeat the mantra you should say to yourself whenever you're about to work on your Social Media (the way we define the term), whatever platforms you use.

S.E.O. and Beyond...

> *Give more than you ask. Across all your Social Media platforms, provide information of real value within your NARROWLY TAILORED MESSAGE. Make it engaging in* **both** *senses of the word. If you're trying to drive traffic to your website or to your other platforms, provide a link and make it clear why it's beneficial for visitors to click on the link. That could mean they'll find useful information at the destination, or it could mean they'll get an incentive. Test and measure. If something's not working, improve it. If it's still not working, remove it. Be relentless. Never, ever, ever give up.*

Section VIII – TEST AND MEASURE

Use Google Analytics

At this point you should have already checked with your web hosting company to see what kind of statistics reporting they offer. And you should be reviewing them every month. But you should also be aware of something called Google Analytics. It's a free service offered by Google that can be integrated into your site relatively easily, and can provide you with all the stats you'll ever need.

Google Analytics tracks which of your pages generates the most hits, which pages people access the most, and where people are leaving your site. You can even set up campaigns to track people through a sign-up process on your site, and find out if people are following through with the entire process or leaving early. If you're even a bit competent with HTML programming, you'll be able to add the code Google needs to track your pages. So stop right here and go sign up for Google Analytics, stat!

Employ Custom Landing Pages

Most basic websites have a pretty similar structure. It generally looks something like this:

> Home
> About Us
> Products & Services
> Contact Us

Those basic pages are fine, but consider this: unless all your products and services are basically the same, they probably all have different keywords that should be optimized. It makes sense to make one or more custom landing pages for **each** idea, product or service you offer. Make sure it's chock full of keywords and helpful information to make it genuinely useful, and not only will your customers find it useful, but the search engines will also take notice.

The real benefit of having a distinct landing page for each of your products is that you can use web stats to track how many people visit. Instead of knowing that 2500 people visited your "Products" page last month, you can now see that 100 visited your "Left Handed Widgets" page and another 700 visited your "Stainless Steel Outdoor Widgets" page. That information could make a huge difference in where to put your marketing and production energy!

Test and Measure

Review Your Stats

The whole point of getting your website to Page One of Google is to attract more visitors to your website. But how do you know if your efforts are working? Hint: check your stats!

Start by checking with your web hosting company. As we mentioned earlier, any decent web hosting company should offer some kind of stats package. It should show how many "hits" and "visits" your site is generating, as well as what sites are referring people to you and what your most popular pages are. If your web hosting company doesn't offer at least these simple stats, it might be time to find a new one!

The point is, you won't know if your activities are working unless you check. Find out how many people have been visiting your site *before* you start working on your internet presence. Compare those numbers with the numbers *after* every month of following our advice. In fact, you should be checking your stats *every* month because they can provide critical clues as to which of your activities is generating the most results for you.

As you might imagine, the trend you want to see is more visitors each month, rather than fewer!

Actually Modify Accordingly

So you've created landing pages for each of your keywords and phrases, which in turn should reflect the products and services that you offer. You've even checked your stats once or twice to see how many people are visiting each of your pages. Great ... now what?

Check again! This isn't a one time deal, it's an ongoing project! You should be tweaking and adjusting your efforts on a regular basis. If hardly anyone is visiting some of your pages, then maybe it's time to reevaluate and make some changes. If hundreds of people are visiting, but no one's buying or even contacting you, then maybe your efforts at attracting new visitors are good, but your website isn't offering those visitors a compelling reason to interact with you or buy what you're selling. How do you know what to change? Well, if you've followed our advice and you really understand your USP, and your marketing really tracks with what your best customers are looking for, then the method you should use is this: if it's working, try to improve it. If it's not working, remove it.

We've had a lot of success with a process we call "A-B Cloning." Other experts probably call it something else, but the name works for us, so we're keeping it! Here's what you do: choose a campaign that seems to be working. Maybe it's a set of Facebook posts that offer an incentive to visitors who sign up for your newsletter.

Test and Measure

It's getting a lot of people to sign up, so you're happy with it, but you wonder if it could do even better. Take a careful look at the content of the campaign. Are there a few words you could change while still staying within your NARROWLY TAILORED MESSAGE? Could you change the photo, the time of day you post, the day on which you post, or the type of humor you use to amp up the engagement1 of the posts? If so, make one change and execute one day's campaign across the relevant platforms.

Pay attention to the results. Is the modified copy performing better than the original? If so, use that until the positive effect tapers off. When it does, clone it again and watch the results. Is the modified copy performing worse than the original? If so, throw it away. Measure, modify, improve or remove. Do it again. And again.

If you really want to do well at the business of improving your marketing, keep a record of your efforts and what performs well. Make guesses about *why* you think some copy performs well and some doesn't. Over time, develop a journal of your thoughts about field-tested marketing ideas, and you'll become an expert at knowing what works and why. If you want to accelerate the process, spend time researching to see if your guesses are in line with the opinions of other experts. As we've said, virtually everything you need to know is available if you search for it. The better you get, the more successful you'll be, and we want a ride on your corporate jet!

Use Eye Tracking

Eye tracking devices can detect what parts of a web page viewers actually look at. If you have the budget and the will to build a truly effective website, you might want to consider hiring an eye tracking expert to review your web pages. But even if you have a very small budget, you can pay attention to the research that's already out there to help maximize the potential of your digital landscape.

Research shows that the most common pattern of viewing websites is a capital "F" pattern. People tend to look at the top of a page and scan to the right, then return to the left side, scan down, then across to the right again, and finally back to the left and down. To ensure that your viewers see the most important content on your page, construct it so that the most important content is laid out like a big capital "F". You can fill in the less-viewed space with less important content or content that builds aesthetics.

If you have the time and budget to actually do some simple eye tracking, there are some economical choices. Most will give you a heatmap based on a limited number of viewers. If you have a larger budget, you can purchase full service eye-tracking software or hire an expert to perform the studies. If you'd like a list of some eye-tracking resources, email us and we'll send you our resource guide absolutely free!

Check Your Backlinks

Hopefully we've explained with enough clarity elsewhere in this book that one of the most important ways Google decides on your importance is by the number of relevant, high-quality websites that link to yours. According to most authorities on the subject, the links that you post on your site matter, too. There's an equation that many webmasters use to determine whether you're giving away more Page Rank than your getting. Although we don't give as much credence to that formula as do many web experts, we still believe that if you have a lot of links on your site that link to dead ends or pages that no longer exist, Google will lower its view of your importance.

The way to prevent being hurt by dead links is to schedule periodic link checks. Once per month should be sufficient for most websites. Click on all the links on your site and make sure they lead somewhere. If you get an error message back, or if the link takes you to a "placeholder" page rather than an active website, you should delete that link from your site.

If you've made a deal with another webmaster to swap links and you accidentally delete their link, don't let it worry you. If they're diligent, they'll discover the missing link and contact you. You can say "Whoops!" and add their link back to your links page!

Check Others' Links to You

If you've read this far, you realize that becoming a major player on the internet can be a lot of work. As you can imagine, others find it a lot of work, too. So don't be surprised if somebody agrees to add a link to your site from their own and either forgets or fails to keep it there when they make changes to their site. Another way people can provide less than optimal help is by adding your link but not adding the anchor text you want. So it makes sense to develop a system to check on the links people have promised you and, for that matter, all the links on the internet that point to your site. You can use one of the free online backlink checkers (just Google "backlink checker"), or you can use Google itself to see who links to you. Just type this into the Google search bar:

links: "mywebsite.com"

You still have to visit the sites to find the links and make sure they actually point to your site, but when you do, check the source code and make sure the link says what you want it to say, and that it's not a "no follow" link (one that's set not to pass on any Page Rank to your site). Whatever you do, be polite when you email people to ask them to add or modify your link. Most webmasters are very amenable to polite requests, and they'll let you know if for some reason they can't accommodate your request.

Be Patient

No doubt you're eager to see your site rocket to Page One immediately. We feel your pain! Even so, patience is a key part of SEO. The world wide web consists of millions of sites with billions of pages, and Google and the other search engines are very busy trying to keep up. Please excuse them if they don't get to your site the instant you make a change!

Results can take time. It'll take time for you to make all the changes needed, time for the search engines to notice, and time for them to adjust your rank. Don't expect results to show up immediately. Keep at it, and have faith that the search engines will eventually notice. It's a lot faster than it used to be, but changes in your Page Rank and search engine placement can take anywhere from a few days to a few months, especially with brand new sites that have no Page Rank and no inbound links on day one.

While you wait, keep busy by making sure all the components we've discussed are in place and that you're providing real value to your visitors. If all else fails, you can spend a little money for pay-per-click advertising on Google and Yahoo! to get some visibility. If you've done everything possible AND you've waited months and you're still nowhere to be found, drop us an email. Our experts can do a detailed analysis of your site for a very reasonable cost!

Section IX – GETTING ON TOP AND STAYING THERE

Check your Competitors' Sites

If a few (or a lot) of your competitors keep getting higher placement results than you, it would be worthwhile to spend time analyzing their sites. There are reasons why they're doing well. Find those reasons, do a better job, and your site will surpass theirs!

Their site may have been around longer. They may have registered their site for longer than you registered yours. They may have better content or better keyword distribution. They may have more quality inbound links. Their Social Media strategy for enticing visitors to their site may be working better. Their URL or page titles may contain more relevant keywords. Their headers may contain more relevant keywords. They may have done a better job at executing the four-in-one optimization we discussed earlier. Chances are, a few of your competitors are working nearly as hard as you are, so be consistent, be persistent, and never give up!

Getting on Top & Staying There

Tell the Search Engines What to Index

We've talked many times about the search engine robots, or "spiders," crawling your site to find keywords and other information so they know what your site's about and how important it is. It turns out you don't have to passively interact with those robots. You can guide them by telling them what to index and what not to index. You do this by using something called a "robots.txt" file.

The first thing most search engine robots do when they crawl your site is search for that file. It's a snippet of text that directs the robots to either look at or not look at parts of your site. You install it in the root of your source code. If you want the robots to be able to access your entire site, your robots.txt file would look like this:

> **User-agent:** *
> **Disallow:**
>
> To block a specific file, you would write this:
> **User-agent:** *
> **Disallow: /lefthandedwidgetsnude/**
>
> And to block your entire site:
> **User-agent:** *
> **Disallow: /**

Add Regular Updates

Keeping your website updated is critical to continued success for several reasons. The first is perhaps the most obvious: people who visit your site want to see things happening, and a six-month old article will make them think your business is not very active. Moreover, although you want to engineer your web pages to include keywords in every logical location, even a page that is highly optimized today will look stale to the search engines in a few months.

And finally, if you think about the approach we recommended for Social Media, you'll recall that we advised you to craft a NARROWLY TAILORED MESSAGE and use it across all your platforms. Well, even the best Social Media campaign has a natural shelf life ... an amount of weeks or months when it will have its optimum effect. After that optimum period, its benefits will start to diminish and it will be time to launch a new campaign.

Besides being diligent about launching and maintaining your campaigns across the MAGNIFICENT SEVEN platforms, we recommend that you set up at least your home page so that the content is changed in one or more ways at least on a weekly basis. That helps to keep repeat visitors interested, keeps the search engines interested, and makes sure time sensitive material on your site doesn't begin to appear dated.

Point Other Domain Names to Your Site

Way back in our section on Domain Names, we talked about how important choosing the right domain name can be. As you'll recall, we pointed out that choosing a keyword-rich domain name gives you an immediate leg up. When a search engine robot is looking for "left handed widgets" and it finds the words in your domain name - LeftHandedWidgets.com - it's going to assume your site is important for that subject matter (all other factors being equal).

Well, suppose you have other ideas, products or services you also want to promote, like "right handed widgets" and "widget removal tools." What's to stop you from registering RightHandedWidgets.com and WidgetRemovalTools.com? Nothing, assuming they're available.

Once you've registered those domains, you can do a variety of useful things with them. You could create a "mirror site" (a copy of your original site). Though the search engines won't give significant Page Rank to the copy site, people who wind up there because they typed in keywords that took them to that domain can still shop just as if they were on the original.

You could also just create a single page under the new domain featuring useful, detailed information about Widget Removal Tools.

S.E.O. and Beyond...

Provide your visitors with a way to go to your main site, or use the specialty page as a "squeeze page," to ask them to opt into your newsletter or other educational process.

Or, if you're creative, you could make the Widget Removal Tools page extremely funny, quirky, surprising, or unique. If the page has enough impact to begin to attract visitors for its own sake, and if you provide a way for them to either go to your main site or enlist in your sales process, you'll increase traffic.

And don't forget that if your secondary domains are useful or entertaining enough, they'll begin to get increased Page Rank, and the links from them to your main site will help propel the Page Rank of your main site higher. This, of course, will result in better search engine results, and you'll own that condo in South Beach in no time!

Link to Your Pages in Your Email Signature

Our clients sometimes ask us if they should have a link to their websites in their email signatures. Our question to them is usually, "why *wouldn't* you want to let people know about your business?"

If you're proud of your idea, product or service, and you sincerely believe in their value, then it makes sense to share them in any way you can, including by providing useful links in your emails. By adding the links to your signature, you make it automatic, so you're promoting your business without thinking about it every time you send an email. Here's how:

> *Some people will see the link title and think of your business. Next time they need what you offer, they're more likely to think of you.*
>
> *Some people will actually click on the link, adding traffic, and hopefully conducting business, on your site.*
>
> *Some people will forward your emails to others, and your link will be put in front of fresh eyes.*

And some webmasters think there is a true SEO boost effect from including links in email accounts in systems like Gmail. After all, we

How to Rocket Your Website to Page One of Google!

know Google is paying attention to the content in your emails because they provide targeted ads on the Gmail page based on keywords they detect. They also display Gmail messages within personal search results. If they're paying this much attention, then they'll notice if a lot of emails contain keywords and links that relate to your NARROWLY TAILORED MESSAGE.

So while we can't say for sure that you'll get a major boost in the search engine results for your website just because you start including a link to it in your emails, we'd be very surprised if there was no benefit whatsoever. And since it's such an easy step, we think it makes sense to try it out.

Become an Authority Website

We started this book with the chapter entitled What Google Wants. And we told you what Google wants, which is content. It's also true that *people* who use the web want content. So it should be pretty clear at this point that the most successful websites deliver content in ways that are appealing to both the search engine robots and to people. It's definitely a popularity contest, and the good news is that, unlike high school, you can have control of how popular you are.

A great way to become popular is to become an authority website. Make it your mission to provide the best information on the internet about your idea, product or service ... and lots of it! Organize the information so that it is easy to navigate, easy to understand, and digestible in small, high impact bites. Seek out others in the internet who recognize the value of the content you provide and who will link back to your site. And tell people in your content, "hey, this is the place to get the most and best information on left handed widgets!"

> *Is becoming an authority website easy? Absolutely not. It will take time to develop all the unique content you need, to get the right collection of backlinks to ensure a robust pagerank and to get lots of traffic.*

S.E.O. and Beyond...

But the good news is that you don't have to try to become an authority website overnight. If you plan well and contruct your website so that it's easy to add new pages (using a great content management system as we mentioned earlier), you can add a little content each day or each week, and over time develop a significant collection of information for your visitors.

As we've tried to make clear, the underlying purpose of your website should be to provide true value to your visitors, whether in the form of pure information, education, resources, the opportunity to be involved in a community, or a convenient place to buy first rate products or services. If you achieve this purpose, people will notice, and you'll become very successful. You can accelerate the rate at which they find you and get on board by following our recommendations for marketing and social media, but at the end of the day, nothing beats being the best resource on the internet in your particular niche.

If you're just starting your website, start with the ultimate goal of becoming an authority website. If you've already owned and maintained a website for years and the results haven't been spectacular, consider making it your mission to start providing more and better content, until you become THE place to go for information about your particular idea, product or service.

Read One Article a Day

The internet is enormous, and it's getting bigger and evolving every day. We recommend building ten or fifteen minutes into every workday to read a bit about SEO, marketing, social media, or effective web design. If you're highly motivated, you can take classes or read other great books like this one. Remember, if you'd like more information or want to dig deeper into some of our topics, we provide a lot more resources in our handy guide. If you'd like a free copy, contact us! We'd love to help. You can find our contact info at:

www.seoannarbor.com

But if you're as busy as we are, you probably want a way to learn and keep on top of new developments. Reading a single article each day is a great way to do that without committing time that should otherwise be spent on income-producing activities.

There are some other positive outcomes as well. You'll learn a lot of internet and marketing vocabulary. You'll learn who the major players are in the internet business, and who to avoid. You'll find ideas about marketing, SEO, and design that you might not have thought of before, and you'll be able to use them in your own business. Read one article a day. In three months, you'll be an expert!

Learn XHTML and CSS

If you really want to get results and be good at this stuff, we recommend that you learn XHTML and CSS. Doing your own coding gives you maximum control over what happens behind the scenes, and as we've said, the source code for your site can help encourage or discourage Google from properly indexing your site. It will help you avoid using the prefab HTML editors that provide limited or no control over code, and which we've found create significant barriers to robust search engine results. Even if you don't end up coding your own site, having a basic understanding of XHTML and CSS will give you the ability to have much more intelligent dialogues with your webmaster, which could save you a lot of time and money.

And web programming, while challenging, isn't rocket surgery. A consistent, steady approach will result in you learning a lot with relatively little pain. If it's worth doing, it's worth doing right, so do yourself a favor and learn XHTML and CSS!

Hire a Professional

And finally, if you've read this book, digested the information, perhaps tried out a few of our recommendations, and, at the end of the day, you realize that your time and mental energy is better spent doing what you do best, then it makes sense to hire a professional.

And when we say "hire a professional," we mean a *professional*. Too many people we've worked with have tried to save money by hiring someone who's cheap or convenient. While we understand the value of money as well as the next guy, we've found that in the long run, our clients spend a lot more money reinventing their sites after some fly-by-night outfit has screwed it up for them.

Your secretary's brother in-law is probably a nice guy. Your neighber with the "Website Design" sign in her front window probably has good intentions. The big, cheap web-hosting companies that let you buy a la carte websites and add plug ins by paying "just a little more" are, well … big, cheap web-hosting companies. They don't care about you and they are very unlikely to give you good counsel on how to integrate all the aspects of web design, SEO, marketing and social media to give you a powerful internet presence with a high return on your marketing investment. And whatever you do, stay away from somebody who says, "I'll fix your CSS just as soon as I finish this course on it at the community college."

S.E.O. and Beyond...

This is probably common sense, but we've seen so many people ignore it, we think it bears repeating here. Check on the credentials of the company you're thinking about working with. Does anybody recommend them? Where are they located? Are you going to be able to sit across the desk from someone in the company who can educate you on your internet needs? If not, what is their process for ensuring good communication with you?

Do they have a portfolio of websites you can inspect? What are their credentials? What's the history of their company? Have they written any books or produced any other information you can study to see whether they seem to know what they're talking about? Do they return calls and emails quickly? Do they seem interested in you and your marketing goals? Are they excited about their work?

We expect that you're enthusiastic and dedicated to your idea, product or service. If you're like us, you want to be able to do what you love, get very good at it, and make a decent living. Chances are, you won't be able to do all that without a pretty good approach to marketing what you do on the internet. You owe it to yourself to take a serious shot at success. If you can't devote the time and energy to making sure you rocket your website to Page One of Google, then hire a professional. You'll be glad you did!

Thank You and Good Luck!

If you've made it this far (or even if you skipped to the end), we want to thank you for the time you put into reading this book. We wish you every success in growing your business to a level that brings you professional satisfaction, a good living, and challenges that are always just beyond what you're already good at!

Please feel free to reach out to us if you'd like further information. We've worked with people in all kinds of businesses, and many just need a little guidance to understand how to promote their businesses better. Just remember, you have to take the first step if you ever want to take the second step, and we've found over and over again that the more seriously our clients take their marketing, the more successful they are. Good marketing can help grow your business, but *great* marketing can take it to places you never imagined. If this books helps you understand a bit better what great marketing on the internet looks like, then our mission has been a success.

Whatever you do ... work hard, stay focused, and never, ever, ever give up on your dreams!

About the Authors

Don E. Prior III is an expert in computer networking and website design. He teaches martial arts and is an entrepreneur who helps small businesses with their computer, network and website needs.

Nicklaus Suino is a writer, martial arts expert, attorney and business consultant who specializes in the mastery process.

Made in the USA
Charleston, SC
15 June 2013